We the Sheeple

How the Media, Congress, and the Courts Undermined Article II — and Redefined Presidential Eligibility

By Lexi Fehr

ISBN: 979-8-950577-43-7

Published by Franklin Publishers

Printed in the United States of America

For permissions, inquiries, or additional copies, contact:

Franklin Publishers

www.franklinpublishers.com

Dedication

Dedicated to all who labored—often quietly and at great personal cost—in the pursuit of justice and fidelity to Article II of the Constitution. Though often ignored or ridiculed, your courage and commitment endure, and your efforts are remembered.

Foreword

In every constitutional order, certain provisions appear settled—words that rest quietly within the text and are rarely examined except in moments of controversy.

Yet, from time to time, a question arises that invites a closer examination, a return to first principles, and a reconsideration of assumptions long taken for granted.

Such questions rarely announce themselves openly. They emerge gradually—in the margins of legal debates, within archival records, in the language of statutes and judicial opinions, and in the persistent curiosity of those who sense that something in the historical record warrants closer attention.

This book begins with one such question.

At the center of this inquiry lies a constitutional phrase that is both familiar and elusive: "natural-born Citizen." Though only a few words long, the phrase carries a history that reaches back through the law of nations, the philosophical traditions of the eighteenth century, and the practical concerns of the generation that framed the Constitution.

For generations, courts, scholars, and public officials have spoken confidently about the requirement. Yet a closer examination of the historical record reveals layers of interpretation that invite renewed consideration.

What did the Founders understand this phrase to mean?

How did that understanding develop within the legal vocabulary of their time?

And how has that understanding been preserved—or transformed—through the processes of law and governance that followed?

The pages that follow offer no easy answers. Instead, they present a careful examination of sources spanning more than two centuries: correspondence among revolutionary leaders, legal treatises that informed their thinking, legislative debates that shaped constitutional doctrine, judicial decisions interpreting its provisions, and archival materials that illuminate moments of controversy. Each document is presented as part of a broader evidentiary landscape in which readers are invited to trace connections, weigh competing interpretations, and consider their implications.

As with any serious legal inquiry, attention to detail matters. A letter written in a particular year, a phrase employed during a debate, or a decision rendered on procedural grounds may acquire significance when viewed within a broader historical context. The task is not merely to recount events, but to examine how they fit within the evolving framework of constitutional interpretation.

The investigation begins in the intellectual world of the Founding generation, where questions of allegiance and political identity were debated with urgency and care. Writers on the law of nations offered frameworks for understanding sovereignty and membership, and American leaders engaged those ideas as they sought to define the character of a new republic. Their writings provide a starting point for understanding how concepts that now appear familiar were once subjects of active deliberation.

From these origins, the inquiry moves forward through subsequent periods of constitutional development, tracing how courts and lawmakers addressed questions of citizenship and qualification. At times, the record reflects continuity; at other times, it reveals tensions that invite further reflection.

In later chapters, the focus turns to more recent controversies that have drawn renewed attention to constitutional requirements. Here, the materials include court filings, public records, and documentary evidence that together form part of an unfolding legal narrative. Readers will encounter instances in which questions were raised, responses were offered, and procedural pathways shaped the course of inquiry.

Along the way, several enduring questions emerge.

What role should historical sources play in interpreting constitutional text? How should institutions respond when contested claims arise? When procedural doctrines limit substantive review, what becomes of the underlying questions? And how does the passage of time influence the meaning attributed to constitutional provisions?

These questions are not merely academic. They speak to the broader process by which a constitutional system maintains fidelity to its foundational commitments while navigating the practical realities of governance.

The study of constitutional law often resembles the reconstruction of a historical record—assembling fragments, examining context, and determining how individual pieces contribute to a larger understanding. It is a process that rewards patience and invites thoughtful engagement.

This volume proceeds in that spirit.

Readers are invited to approach these materials with the same care that guides judicial inquiry: to examine the sources, consider the arguments, and reflect upon the questions that emerge. The purpose is not to prescribe conclusions, but to provide a framework within which those conclusions may be thoughtfully reached.

In a republic governed by written law, the act of examination is itself an affirmation of constitutional principle. The enduring vitality of the Constitution depends not only upon institutions, but also upon a willingness to engage seriously and honestly with its text and history.

Every meaningful investigation begins with uncertainty.

What follows is an invitation to explore a historical record, follow its threads across time, consider the questions it raises, and reflect upon what it may reveal about the continuing project of constitutional self-government. Some questions, once asked, do not easily fade. This book invites readers to consider them carefully.

My Research Assistant
Mr. Otis

Preface

I wrote this book after sixteen years of pursuing what I believe to be a fundamental constitutional truth, one that has been overlooked, misunderstood, or dismissed by those entrusted with safeguarding our laws.

During that time, I repeatedly encountered a troubling reality: significant questions about the meaning of citizenship and presidential eligibility were often dismissed without meaningful engagement, while the historical record remained largely unexplored in public discourse. This work is my effort to place that record before the American people.

From the beginning, my concern has not been about personalities or political parties, but about fidelity to the Constitution. If the Constitution establishes qualifications for the presidency, those qualifications must be understood as the Framers intended — not reshaped by convenience, assumption, or modern reinterpretation detached from history.

What began as a simple question evolved into years of study. I immersed myself in the Declaration of Independence, the Constitution, the records of the Constitutional Convention, the Federalist Papers, and the writings and correspondence of the Founding Generation. I examined the Articles of Confederation, early naturalization laws, and debates from the Reconstruction Congress, including the Civil Rights Act of 1866 and the adoption of the Thirteenth, Fourteenth, and Fifteenth Amendments. I read judicial opinions spanning more than two centuries, along with historical commentaries addressing citizenship, allegiance, and sovereignty.

Along the way, I worked with others who shared an interest in these questions, and together we sought to raise awareness through lawful channels — contacting representatives, engaging with media outlets, and pursuing legal remedies. Yet time and again, the evidence itself was seldom addressed directly. Instead, discussion often gave way to dismissal or misunderstanding.

It is also important to understand how these questions became personal to me, the story behind this book, and the path that led me here. What follows is not only the result of years of research, but also the personal journey of living through what I believe has been a constitutional crisis while much of the nation remained unaware.

For nearly two decades, I carried a growing conviction that something fundamental had gone wrong — that the meaning of citizenship and presidential eligibility had been quietly altered, even as most Americans continued to trust that the Constitution's safeguards remained intact. Over time, the weight of that realization became impossible for me to ignore.

My journey began long before I ever imagined writing a book. In high school, during a civics lesson on Article II of the Constitution and presidential eligibility, my teacher posed a question that would later shape decades of research: What is a natural-born citizen? When I was unable to answer, he explained that a natural-born citizen is one born in a country to parents who are themselves citizens, grounding the definition in principles of natural law.

At the time, the explanation seemed straightforward, yet the concept lingered in my mind long after the class ended. Looking back, I believe that moment planted a seed — one that would gradually shape the course of my life in ways I could not yet understand.

Over the past sixteen years, I have tested that definition against historical records, founding-era writings, and constitutional sources, examining whether the understanding presented in that classroom reflected the legal and intellectual framework familiar to the Founding generation. Repeatedly, the evidence appeared to support the principle first introduced to me in that civics lesson.

In 1989, I experienced an event that profoundly changed my perspective on life and my sense of purpose. A catastrophic medical error sent me into full cardiac arrest. At one point, I heard someone say, "We've lost her." After approximately four minutes, my heart was restarted.

When I later awoke in recovery, I carried with me a deep sense that I had been given more time for a reason, that my life had not been spared by accident. In the years that followed, that feeling never completely left me.

As my research deepened and the constitutional questions surrounding citizenship became clearer, I began to believe that documenting this history was part of the purpose for which God had spared my life, an obligation grounded in both conscience and the principles of natural law to pursue what I understood to be the truth and to bring that evidence forward.

This book, therefore, represents more than an academic investigation. It is the result of years of study, reflection, and conviction, an effort to assemble historical sources, legislative records, and judicial statements that illuminate how earlier generations understood the relationship between birth, allegiance, and political membership.

I recognize that the subject can be controversial. Yet controversy alone does not diminish the importance of carefully examining constitutional questions. On the contrary, the durability of our constitutional system depends upon a willingness to revisit foundational principles and ensure that our understanding remains grounded in text and history.

The Founders spoke often of natural law, the law of nations, and the necessity of maintaining a government bound by fixed rules rather than shifting preferences. The Reconstruction Congress confronted directly the failures exposed by the Civil War and sought to clarify citizenship in statutory and constitutional language. Courts, legislators, and scholars have continued to interpret these provisions over time, sometimes in harmony with earlier understandings and sometimes in tension with them.

This book traces that development chronologically so that readers can examine the historical record for themselves.

I do not claim that every reader will agree with my conclusions. What I hope is that readers will approach the evidence with an open mind and a shared commitment to understanding the Constitution as a living inheritance, one that demands both respect and careful study.

Ultimately, this book is an appeal to civic responsibility. The preservation of constitutional government does not rest solely with courts or elected officials; it rests with an informed citizenry willing to engage seriously with the principles that define our Republic.

If this work encourages even a small number of readers to examine the historical record more closely, then its purpose will have been fulfilled.

My sincere hope is that by bringing these materials together, this work contributes, however modestly, to a renewed conversation about constitutional meaning, national sovereignty, and the enduring importance of the rule of law.

Acknowledgements

I would like to express my sincere gratitude to those whose research, dedication, encouragement, and support helped make this book possible.

My deepest thanks go to Noah Cohen, whose support, counsel, and belief in this project helped bring it from initial concept to publication. His guidance throughout the publishing process was invaluable, and his confidence in the importance of this work is deeply appreciated.

A special thank-you is owed to Chloe Benavidez, whose exceptional editorial guidance, professionalism, and patience helped transform this manuscript into a far more polished and accessible work. Her keen attention to detail and unwavering dedication to the craft of editing greatly enhanced the final product.

I am also grateful to Dr. Orly Taitz for her tireless efforts in pursuing questions of presidential eligibility and for her unwavering willingness to challenge accepted narratives through litigation, research, and public advocacy.

I also extend my appreciation to Montgomery Sibley for his legal work, persistence, and principled commitment to examining constitutional questions that many believed should not be ignored.

Special recognition is due to Sharon Rondeau, publisher of The Post & Email, for her years of meticulous reporting, careful documentation, and invaluable preservation of information that might otherwise have been overlooked or forgotten. Her dedication to independent investigative journalism has created an important public record for researchers and citizens alike.

I am likewise grateful to retired Commander Charles Kerchner of ProtectOurLiberty.org for his steadfast commitment to constitutional principles and his extensive research into citizenship, presidential eligibility, and the historical foundations of American law.

Finally, I extend my gratitude to all those who continue to ask difficult questions, pursue historical truth, and work to preserve the Constitution and the rule of law for future generations. Whatever differences of opinion may exist, the continued pursuit of truth, open inquiry, and constitutional fidelity remains essential to the health of our Republic.

Introduction

What if one of the Constitution's most important safeguards has been quietly ignored—not through open defiance, but through misunderstanding, neglect, and the gradual erosion of historical memory?

For those who believe the question of natural-born citizenship and presidential eligibility was settled long ago, the evidence presented in this book may come as a surprise. Imagine discovering years after an election that a candidate who did not satisfy the Constitution's requirements was permitted to appear on the presidential ballot—and not only permitted, but elected twice. Many assume such questions have already been thoroughly examined and resolved. Yet the historical record tells a different story, one that has often been overlooked, misunderstood, or dismissed by the very institutions charged with examining it.

At its core, this book explores a fundamental constitutional distinction between two categories of citizens: natural-born citizens and naturalized citizens. According to the historical understanding examined in these pages, natural-born citizens are those who acquire citizenship by birth, while naturalized citizens acquire it through statute or legal process. The distinction is not merely semantic. It lies at the center of the Constitution's presidential eligibility requirements and raises important questions about how citizenship has been understood throughout American history.

The evidence assembled here is drawn from primary sources, including federal statutes, congressional debates, official government records, Supreme Court decisions, diplomatic documents, and the writings of the Founding generation. Collectively, these materials illuminate how earlier Americans understood citizenship, allegiance, and the constitutional term "natural-born Citizen."

These sources have long been publicly available. Yet despite their availability, the subject has often been treated superficially or dismissed without sustained examination. Public discussion has frequently relied upon assumptions, secondary interpretations, or incomplete analysis rather than a comprehensive review of the historical record itself.

To place the evidence in its proper context, this book proceeds chronologically. It begins with the intellectual foundations that shaped the Founding era and then follows the development of citizenship and eligibility through constitutional debates, legislative enactments, judicial decisions, and modern legal controversies. Because the evidence unfolds over time, some of the most significant documents and developments appear later in the narrative. Readers are therefore encouraged to follow the historical progression from beginning to end.

The goal is not merely to recount events, but to allow the documentary record to speak for itself. By examining the sources in sequence, patterns emerge that help illuminate how concepts of citizenship, allegiance, and political membership were understood, debated, and applied across generations.

As this study progressed, it led me to questions—and ultimately conclusions—that I did not initially anticipate. What began as an effort to better understand the historical meaning of citizenship evolved into a broader examination of how constitutional principles are interpreted and applied in modern circumstances.

Although the Obama eligibility controversy brought renewed public attention to these issues, the constitutional questions explored in this book extend far beyond any single individual. They concern the broader evolution of the meaning of "natural-born Citizen" and the methods by which constitutional language is interpreted over time.

The purpose of this work is not to ask readers to accept any conclusion at the outset. Rather, it is to present the historical record, documentary evidence, and procedural developments in a manner that allows readers to evaluate the issues for themselves. At the same time, intellectual honesty requires me to acknowledge that this inquiry ultimately led me to conclusions that differ from some prevailing interpretations. Those conclusions will be explained as the historical record unfolds.

The chapters that follow trace the path of that inquiry from foundational principles to contemporary events. They explain how the evidence was gathered, how the relevant questions were examined, and how particular conclusions emerged from the research process.

The early chapters focus on the intellectual and legal foundations that shaped the Founders' understanding of citizenship, allegiance, and the law of nations. By examining the writings, debates, and legal traditions familiar to the generation that drafted the Constitution, it becomes possible to better understand the original context in which the term "natural-born Citizen" appeared.

The discussion then moves forward through Reconstruction-era legislation, judicial decisions, and later political developments. This progression is deliberate. Only by first understanding the historical framework can later controversies be evaluated within their proper constitutional context.

The final portion of the book examines more recent events in which questions concerning presidential eligibility were raised before courts and public institutions. Drawing upon court filings, public records, and documentary evidence, these chapters explore how such questions were addressed procedurally, politically, and legally.

Viewed as a whole, the historical record and modern developments form a continuous narrative that invites readers to consider how constitutional principles articulated in the eighteenth century have been interpreted in the centuries that followed.

For the reader's convenience, a Table of Authorities appears below. This compilation demonstrates that the discussion rests upon original documents and historical evidence rather than conjecture or political rhetoric. It provides a roadmap to the sources informing the analysis and enables readers to verify the material independently.

What follows is the documentary foundation upon which this study rests.

Table of Authorities:

I. Constitutional Provisions

U.S. Const. art. I, § 8, cl. 10

U.S. Const. art. II, § 1, cl. 5

U.S. Const. art. VI (Supremacy Clause)

U.S. Const. amend. XIV

II. Federal Statutes

Naturalization Act of 1790

Naturalization Act of 1795

Civil Rights Act of 1866 (Apr. 9, 1866)

Revised Statutes of 1873–1874, Title XXV, § 1992

Enforcement Act of 1870

Chinese Exclusion Act (1882)

British Nationality Act of 1948

III. Supreme Court Cases

The Venus, 12 U.S. (8 Cranch) 253 (1814)

The Nereide, 13 U.S. (9 Cranch) 388 (1815)

Wheaton v. Peters, 33 U.S. (8 Pet.) 591 (1834)

Dred Scott v. Sandford, 60 U.S. (19 How.) 393 (1857)

The Slaughter-House Cases, 83 U.S. (16 Wall.) 36 (1873)

Minor v. Happersett, 88 U.S. (21 Wall.) 162 (1874)

Elk v. Wilkins, 112 U.S. 94 (1884)

United States v. Wong Kim Ark, 169 U.S. 649 (1898)

Banco Nacional de Cuba v. Sabbatino, 376 U.S. 398 (1964)

IV. Congressional Debates & Records

Congressional Globe (39th Congress)

Bingham Remarks (Mar. 9, 1866)

Trumbull Remarks (May 30, 1866)

Howard Remarks (1866)

Journal of the Senate (1794 order for Vattel)

V. Founding-Era Documents

Vattel, *The Law of Nations* (1758 ed.)

James Otis, *The Rights of the British Colonies Asserted and Proved* (1764)

John Adams, *Diary Entries* (1763, 1765, 1774)

Samuel Adams, *Rights of the Colonists* (1772)

George Washington Letter (1773)

Thomas Jefferson, *Summary View of the Rights of British America* (1774)

Fairfax Resolves (1774)

Declaration and Resolves of the First Continental Congress (1774)

Ben Franklin Letter to Charles Dumas (1775)

Virginia Declaration of Rights (1776)

Declaration of Independence (1776)

Treaty of Paris (1783)

Federalist Papers

VI. Diplomatic & Treaty Sources

American Diplomatic Code Manual

Treaty of Washington (1874)

VII. Historical and Documentary Sources

Colonial Society of Massachusetts (1917)

Kenyan Hansard - Parliamentary record (Kenya) (Mar. 25, 2010, statement)

Reader's Guide — Why Chronology Matters

This book is organized deliberately in chronological order.

Questions concerning citizenship, allegiance, and the meaning of the term "natural-born Citizen" cannot be fully understood through isolated quotations or modern interpretations alone. They must be examined within the historical sequence in which the relevant ideas developed—from the Founding era, through Reconstruction, and into later judicial and political debates.

Constitutional meaning is often illuminated not by a single document, but by the accumulation of evidence across time: letters, legislative debates, statutes, court decisions, and public controversies. Each chapter builds upon the last, allowing readers to see how particular principles emerged, evolved, and were later interpreted.

For that reason, some of the most significant evidence does not appear at the beginning of the book. The early chapters establish the intellectual and legal foundations of the inquiry, while later chapters examine how those principles were applied, debated, and challenged in practice. Reading the material in sequence provides a fuller understanding of the historical continuity that connects these events.

This chronological approach also helps distinguish among three important sources of authority:

• The philosophical foundations reflected in natural law and the law of nations.

• The legislative understanding expressed through statutes and congressional debates.

• The judicial interpretations articulated by courts and legal commentators.

By proceeding step by step through the historical record, readers can observe how these layers interact, reinforce one another, and at times come into tension.

The purpose of this book is not merely to present conclusions, but to allow the evidence to unfold within its historical context. Each document, case, and debate forms part of an evolving narrative that invites careful consideration rather than quick judgment.

Table of Contents

I

Natural Law and the Founding Generation

The intellectual foundations of citizenship, allegiance, and the Law of Nations.

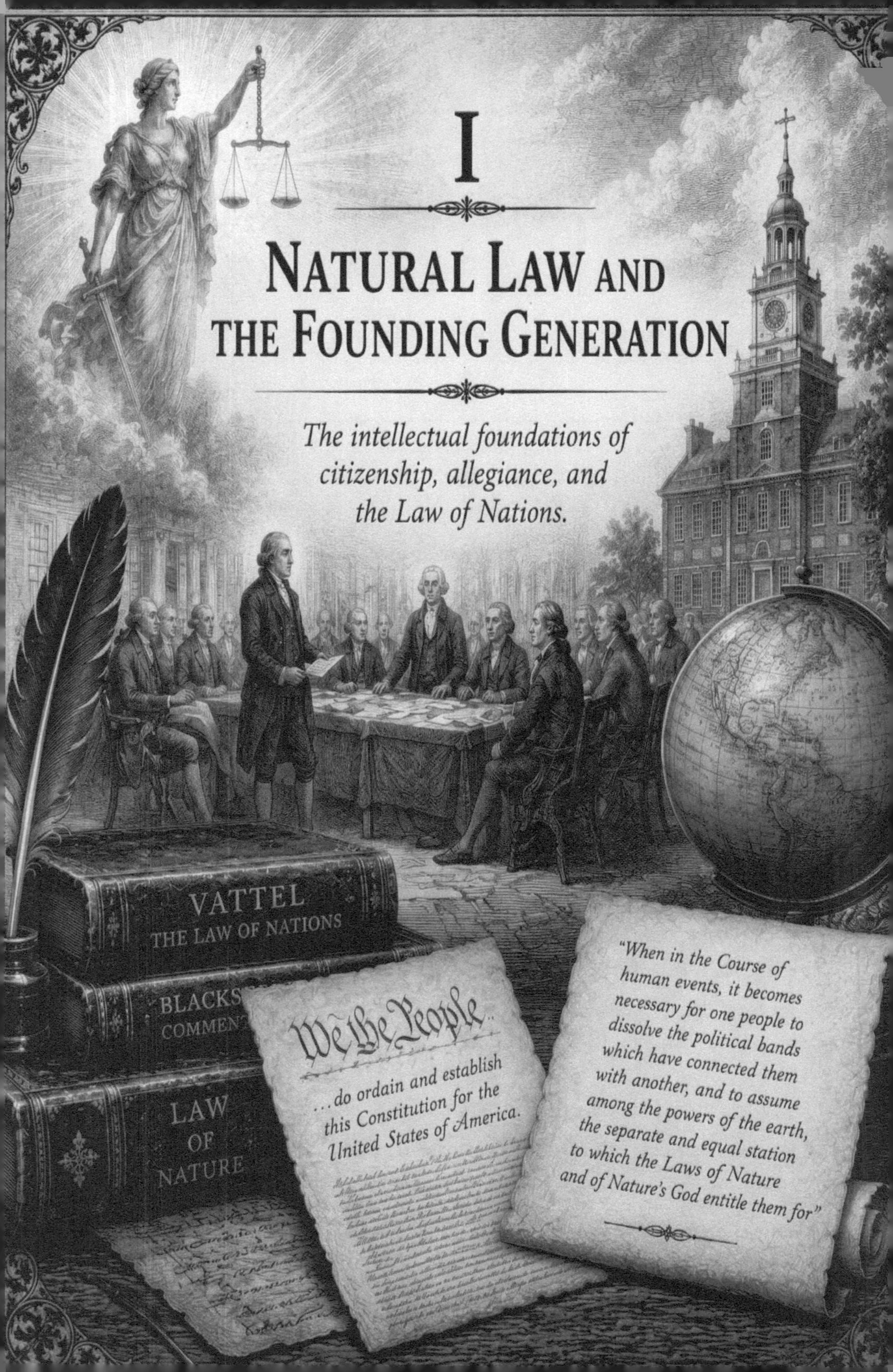

I

Natural Law and the Founding Generation

The intellectual foundations of citizenship, allegiance, and The Law of Nations

The central question addressed in this book is not whether the term "natural-born citizen" appears in the Constitution; it clearly does, but how the Founders understood and defined it.[1] As with any serious inquiry into constitutional meaning, the proper starting point is the intellectual and legal framework familiar to the generation that drafted and ratified the document.

In 2008, renewed public attention to presidential eligibility prompted me to begin a focused examination of Article II, Section 1, which provides:

"No Person except a natural-born Citizen, or a Citizen of the United States, at the time of the Adoption of this Constitution, shall be eligible to the Office of President..."[2]

This provision raised a critical historical question: what did the Founders mean by the term "natural-born citizen"? Unlike modern discourse, saturated with partisan commentary, opinion journalism, and speculative analysis, the historical record is comparatively restrained. Primary sources from the founding and Reconstruction

1 Jack N. Rakove, Original Meanings: Politics and Ideas in the Making of the Constitution (New York: Alfred A. Knopf, 1996).
2 U.S. Const. art. II, § 1, cl. 5.

eras consist largely of official government documents, legislative debates, judicial opinions, and the private writings of those directly involved in the formation of the Republic.

By examining Founders' diaries, congressional records, early statutes, and Supreme Court decisions, it becomes possible to trace the intellectual origin of the term "natural-born citizen." Contemporary political disputes do not drive this inquiry; rather, it is the historical evidence itself.

The conceptual foundation of this investigation lies in natural law, a framework that historically informed the very definitions of citizenship the Founders embraced. By returning to these first principles, we can establish the intellectual landscape from which the constitutional term 'natural-born citizen' was derived.[3]

Early American understandings of natural law and the "Laws of Nature" are well documented in colonial-era pamphlets and public speeches,[4] particularly in the Massachusetts Colony. Boston patriots routinely invoked these principles in political discourse, treating natural law not as abstract philosophy but as the governing framework for rights, allegiance, and political membership.

Many of the Boston patriots who articulated early American conceptions of natural law were members of the Sons of Liberty,[5] a clandestine political organization formed in opposition to British rule. Among its members were James Otis, John Hancock, Paul Revere, Patrick Henry, John Adams, and Samuel Adams[6], figures who would become central to the ideological groundwork of the American Revolution.

John Adams later described James Otis as "the most important

---

3 Emer de Vattel, *The Law of Nations;* bk. 1, chap. 19, § 212. (London, 1758).

4 Bernard Bailyn, *The Ideological Origins of the American Revolution* (Cambridge, MA: Harvard University Press, 1967).

5 https://www.bostonteapartyship.com/sons-of-liberty

6 Pauline Maier, From Resistance to Revolution: Colonial Radicals and the Development of American Opposition to Britain, 1765–1776 (New York: Alfred A. Knopf, 1972).

American of the 1760s,"[7] crediting him as both a mentor and a principal intellectual force behind the colonial resistance. Otis was responsible for drafting and transmitting letters to England that articulated colonial grievances and asserted the colonists' rights under principles that transcended parliamentary authority.

In 1761, Otis gave his most influential expression to these ideas when he challenged the British-imposed Writs of Assistance. These general search warrants authorized customs officials to enter private homes without cause. Arguing before the Boston court, Otis invoked natural law as a higher authority,[8] contending that such writs were void even if sanctioned by Parliament because they violated inherent rights belonging to the people.

Otis's argument illustrates how natural law served as a governing principle in early American political thought, defining the limits of authority and the conditions of legitimate membership in the political community. These principles did not remain abstract theory; they were repeatedly invoked to justify resistance, articulate rights, and define the relationship between the individual and the state.

Otis expanded these ideas in 1764 when he published the pamphlet *The Rights of the British Colonies Asserted and Proved* [9] in Boston. Widely circulated in the colonies, the work became one of the most influential natural-law arguments of the pre-Revolutionary period. In it, Otis grounded colonial rights not in parliamentary grant but in immutable principles derived from nature itself. This formulation would later echo in the Declaration of Independence's assertion that men are "endowed by their Creator with certain unalienable Rights."[10]

---

7 John Adams, in The Works of John Adams, ed. Charles Francis Adams, vol. 10 (Boston: Little, Brown, 1856)

8 John Adams, notes on the Writs of Assistance argument (1761), Massachusetts Historical Society.

9 James Otis, The Rights of the British Colonies Asserted and Proved (Boston: Edes & Gill, 1764).

10 The Declaration of Independence, July 4, 1776.

Otis stated plainly that "the law of nature was not of man's making, nor is it in his power to mend it, or alter its course. He can only perform and keep or disobey and break it."[11] This framing placed natural law above all forms of civil authority, including statutes enacted by Parliament.

Significantly, Otis did not treat natural law as a purely philosophical abstraction. In his pamphlet and related speeches, he cited Vattel by name on multiple occasions, explicitly linking colonial grievances to the law of nations. References to the "law of nature" appear repeatedly throughout the text, including a dedicated section entitled "Of the Natural Rights of Colonists," in which Otis wrote, "The colonists are by the law of nature free born, as indeed all men are, white or black."[12]

Elsewhere, Otis elaborated that the natural rights of the colonists flowed from their status as men, "the common children of the same Creator,"[13] who exist in a state of equality and freedom under the laws of nature and reason unless and until they form a political society. Authority, he argued, derives its legitimacy only insofar as it conforms to those higher principles.

Otis further maintained that no accumulation of time or custom could supersede natural law, writing that "there can be no prescription old enough to supersede the law of nature, and the grant of God Almighty."[14] Governments that deviated from truth, justice, and equity, regardless of their form, he warned, "verge towards tyranny" and are subject to resistance by the people.

Throughout his work, Otis treated natural law as universally binding, equally applicable to democracies, aristocracies, and monarchies, and as the foundation upon which lawful government must rest. In doing so, he articulated a conception of political order

11 James Otis, The Rights of the British Colonies Asserted and Proved (Boston: Edes & Gill, 1764). https://www.loc.gov/exhibits/creating-the-united-states/interactives/declaration-of-independence/slavery/enlarge4-transcribe.html

12 Ibid.

13 Ibid., 28

14 https://billofrightsinstitute.org/activities/handout-c-in-his-own-words-james-otis-on-natural-rights/

in which rights, liberty, and membership in society were governed by pre-existing natural principles rather than legislative convenience.

James Otis's influence extended well beyond his own writings and courtroom arguments. He played a critical role in mentoring many of the figures who would later become central to the American founding, shaping their understanding of natural law, resistance to arbitrary power, and the moral limits of political authority.[15]

Otis's public career was tragically cut short in 1769, when he was struck on the head by a British tax collector's cane during an altercation at the British Coffee House in Boston.[16] The injury left him mentally and physically impaired, preventing his continued participation in public life and ultimately precluding his involvement in the drafting and signing of the Declaration of Independence.[17] In 1783, Otis was killed after being struck by lightning while observing a thunderstorm.[18] Although he died before the adoption of the Constitution, his intellectual contributions have led historians to regard him as a Founding Father in substance if not in formal designation.[19]

Later scholars have consistently recognized the centrality of natural law in Otis's thought. In the *Law, the State and the International Community* (1939), James Scott references Otis's 1764 speech opposing the Writs of Assistance and characterizes Parliament's interference with colonial rights as a violation of the "law of nature."[20] Scott's analysis situates Otis within a broader transatlantic legal tradition that treated natural law as a binding constraint on sovereign power.

15 Bernard Bailyn, The Ideological Origins of the American Revolution (Cambridge, MA: Harvard University Press, 1967), discussion of Otis's influence.

16 Pauline Maier, From Resistance to Revolution: Colonial Radicals and the Development of American Opposition to Britain, 1765–1776 (New York: Knopf, 1972), Otis's biography section (pg 188).

17 Colonial Society of Massachusetts, The Caning of James Otis Jr., 324

18 Guy Carleton Lee, ed., Orators of America, pt. I (New York: G. P. Putnam's Sons, 1902), 21.

19 Bernard Bailyn's The Ideological Origins of the American Revolution (1967) characterization of Otis's role

20 James Brown Scott, *Law, the State, and the International Community* (New York: Columbia University Press, 1939), treatment of Otis and "law of nature" (pg 265)

This interpretation is reinforced in discussions of colonial political theory that trace the transmission of natural-law principles from revolutionary agitators to formal declarations. In examining the intellectual climate of the period, scholars note that phrases such as "the immutable laws of God and nature"[21] were repeatedly employed by Samuel Adams and, at his instigation, incorporated into the Declaration of the First Continental Congress in 1774.[22]

Professor Ernest Barker, in his translation of Otto Gierke's *Natural Law and the Theory of Society*, explains that in the Puritan atmosphere of North America, the secular law of nature recovered its theological foundation. Samuel Adams, Barker observes, claimed for the colonists "the indefeasible rights with which God and Nature have invested them,"[23] grounding political resistance in both moral and divine authority.

Barker notes that this intellectual lineage culminated in the Declaration of Independence, which asserts that the American people are entitled to a "separate and equal station" under "the Laws of Nature and of Nature's God."[24] Far from being a rhetorical flourish, this formulation reflected an established legal and philosophical framework familiar to colonial lawyers.

Significantly, Barker remarks that it is "curious to reflect that Vattel's work on the principles of Natural Law was currently used in the sodalitas of the Boston lawyers"[25]—a professional and intellectual circle in which Otis, Adams, and their contemporaries operated. The presence of Vattel's *Law of Nations* within this milieu underscores the extent to which natural law and the law of nations

21 Samuel Adams, "The Rights of the Colonists": The Report of the Committee of Correspondence to the Boston Town Meeting, November 20, 1772.

22 Journals of the Continental Congress, 1774–1789, ed. Worthington Chauncey Ford et al. (Washington, DC: Government Printing Office, 1904–37), especially "Declaration and Resolves of the First Continental Congress," October 14, 1774.

23 Otto Gierke, Natural Law and the Theory of Society, 1500 to 1800, trans. Ernest Barker (Cambridge: Cambridge University Press, 1934), xlvii, "Translator's Introduction."

24 The Declaration of Independence, July 4, 1776.

25 Otto von Gierke, Natural Law and the Theory of Society 1500–1800, trans. Ernest Barker, with an introduction by Ernst Troeltsch (Boston: Beacon Press, 1958), xlvii.

informed early American conceptions of rights, sovereignty, and political membership.

"It is perhaps not so curious as Professor Barker suggests that Vattel's work should have been quoted"[26] by American revolutionaries. By the time of the Declaration, Vattel's treatise was widely regarded as a standard authority on international law and natural law alike.[27] First published in 1758, it was a relatively recent work yet one that had already achieved broad circulation and esteem throughout the Western world.

Vattel's influence was further amplified by its accessibility. The work was translated into English early, making it readily available to American statesmen without reliance on French sources. Copies of the English edition were known to be in circulation among colonial leaders,[28] where the text functioned not merely as a philosophical reference but as a practical guide to questions of sovereignty, allegiance, and political legitimacy.

Additional evidence of Vattel's prominence appears in the actions of Charles William Frederic Dumas, a Swiss intellectual living in Amsterdam and sympathetic to the American cause. In 1775, Dumas sent copies of *The Law of Nations* to Benjamin Franklin,[29] accompanied by a prefatory introduction. Franklin, in turn, distributed the volumes to influential institutions and individuals, including members of Congress, the Carpenter's Library in Philadelphia, and the College of Massachusetts Bay, now Harvard University.

In a letter dated December 19, 1775, Franklin acknowledged receipt of the books and remarked that others had "reached their destinations." He further noted that Congress found the work timely,

26 James Brown Scott, Law, the State, and the International Community (New York: Columbia University Press, 1939-1940), pg 266

27 1. Christov T. Receptions of Vattel in Nineteenth- and Twentieth-Century International Law. In: Schröder P, ed. Concepts and Contexts of Vattel's Political and Legal Thought. Cambridge University Press; 2021:277-295.

28 William Ossipow, Dominik Gerber, The Reception of Vattel's *Law of Nations* in the American Colonies: Volume 57, Issue 4, December 2017, Pages 521–555, https://doi.org/10.1093/ajlh/njx023

29 Benjamin Franklin to Charles Guillaume Frédéric Dumas, December 9, 1775, Founders Online, National Archives.

observing that "it came to us in good season, when the circumstances of a rising State make it necessary frequently to consult *The Law of Nations*."[30] This correspondence confirms that Vattel's treatise was not merely owned, but actively consulted during the formative period of American independence.

By 1780, only a few years after Dumas's gift, *The Law of Nations* had become a textbook in American colleges[31]—at a time when the colonies were still regarded, at least formally, as part of the British imperial system. The sustained reliance on Vattel by American statesmen and jurists underscores the role of natural law as a governing framework for defining sovereignty, political membership, and the conditions under which legitimate authority arises.

My research into natural law and the American founding revealed frequent references to the phrase "the Laws of Nature." Across these sources, the name Emmerich de Vattel appeared repeatedly, directing my attention towards his influential work, *The Law of Nations*.

While tracing the reach of Vattel's ideas in the American colonies, I discovered an early advertisement announcing the importation of *The Law of Nations* into New York. Published in the New-York Gazette on November 29, 1762,[32] the notice confirms that the book was available to colonial readers well before the American Revolution.

The advertisement was placed by Garrat Noel, a New York bookseller who emigrated from Spain in 1750 and is often identified as the city's first professional bookseller. That Vattel's *Law of Nations* was on Noel's shelves as early as 1762 demonstrates that foundational works of natural law were not merely abstract European theories, but accessible texts circulating within the intellectual life of the colonies.

---

30 Benjamin Franklin to Charles Guillaume Frédéric Dumas, Dec. 19, 1775, in The Papers of Benjamin Franklin (or Founders Online), quotation re "good season" and "consult the law of nations."

31 The Study of International Law in American Law Schools: A Brief History https://law.marquette.edu/facultyblog/category/legal-education/

32 *"The Law of Nations,"* advertisement, New-York Gazette, November 29, 1762.

As early as 1763, John Adams, the future President of the United States, explicitly referenced Emmerich de Vattel in his personal diary. Writing from Braintree on February 1, 1763, Adams lamented his failure to engage more deeply with Vattel's work, noting that "The Idea of M. de Vattel indeed, scowling and frowning, haunted me."[33]

This passage is significant. At a minimum, it demonstrates Adams's familiarity with Vattel's ideas and his recognition of their importance. The language suggests that *The Law of Nations* weighed heavily on his mind, indicating prior exposure and serious intellectual consideration well before the American Revolution.

In 1765, Adams again cited Vattel, specifically referencing a rule from *The Law of Nations* that emphasizes following an author's intention over their literal words, a principle Adams deemed of 'great use to judges.' Establishing this early reliance on Vattel's interpretive rules provides the necessary context for how the Founders later applied these definitions to the Constitution.

In that passage, Adams wrote that "in unforeseen cases... we should rather follow [the author's] intention than his words, and interpret the act as he himself would have interpreted it," adding that "This rule is of great use to judges."[34] Adams explicitly attributed this principle to Vattel, underscoring the jurist's influence on his developing views of legal interpretation.

The Massachusetts Historical Society preserves the full text of Adams's 1765 diary entry and can be consulted in Diary of John Adams, Volume I.

As documented in the records of the Colonial Society of Massachusetts, multiple editions of Emmerich de Vattel's *Law of*

33 John Adams, diary entry, February 1, 1763, in Diary and Autobiography of John Adams, vol. 1, ed. L. H. Butterfield (Cambridge, MA: Harvard University Press, 1961). https://ia601508.us.archive.org/15/items/in.ernet.dli.2015.110866/2015.110866.Diary-And-Autobiography-Of-John-Adams-Vol-I_text.pdf

34 John Adams, diary entry (1765), in Diary and Autobiography of John Adams, vol. 1 (Butterfield ed.), https://www.masshist.org/publications/adams-papers/index.php/view/ADMS-01-01-02-0008-0001-0001

Nations had reached the American colonies by the mid-eighteenth century.[35] Evidence indicates that copies were circulating as early as 1764.

One such copy, a French edition published in 1758 and translated into English in 1760, was received at Harvard College before 1773. Another influential edition, translated into English and published at The Hague in 1775, included an extensive preface and explanatory notes explicitly connecting Vattel's principles to the American cause.

The Publications of the Colonial Society of Massachusetts further record that this 1775 Hague edition was edited by Charles Guillaume Frédéric Dumas, who acted as an intermediary between European publishers and American colonial leaders. As noted earlier, sent copies of his newly edited edition to Benjamin Franklin in Philadelphia, one of which Franklin forwarded to the Library Company of Philadelphia, another to Franklin himself, and a third to Harvard College.[36]

In October of 1775, Franklin donated one of these copies to the Library Company of Philadelphia, noting that members of the First Continental Congress frequently used it.[37] The Harvard copy, later identified as Dumas's own, contained handwritten French commentary in the margins, likely added before it reached the College. This manuscript commentary was later identified by Worthington C. Ford as belonging to Dumas himself.

These records demonstrate that Vattel's *Law of Nations* was not merely known in the abstract, but physically present, actively read, annotated, and circulated among colonial institutions and leading figures during the formative years of the American founding.

---

35 Colonial Society of Massachusetts, Transactions of the Colonial Society of Massachusetts, vol. 20 (Boston: Colonial Society of Massachusetts, 1918), pg5.

36 Ibid. (Dumas/Franklin/Harvard chain).

37 "Benjamin Franklin to Charles-Guillaume-Frédéric Dumas, 9 December 1775," Founders Online, National Archives, https://founders.archives.gov/documents/Franklin/01-22-02-0172 [Original source: The Papers of Benjamin Franklin, vol. 22, March 23, 1775, through October 27, 1776, ed. William B. Willcox. New Haven and London:: Yale University Press, 1982, pp. 287–291.]

Shown below is the title page of the 1758 edition of *The Law of Nations*[38] by Emmerich de Vattel. The same work circulated among colonial leaders and institutions during the founding era. The full title, *The Law of Nations, or, Principles of the Law of Nature: Applied to the Conduct and Affairs of Nations and Sovereigns*, is itself revealing, explicitly linking the law of nations to natural law.

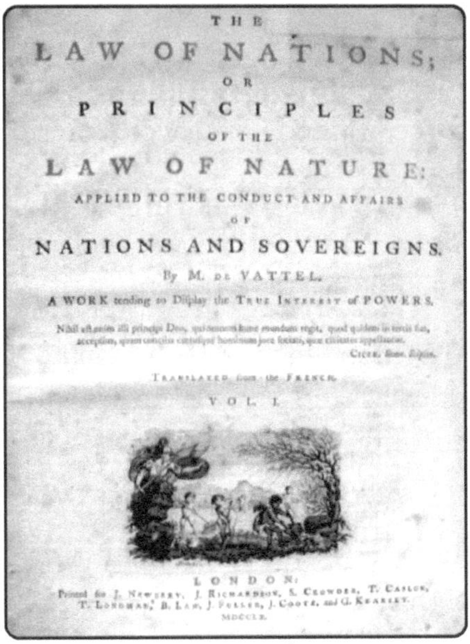

THE

LAW OF NATIONS;

OR

PRINCIPLES

OF THE

LAW OF NATURE:

APPLIED TO THE CONDUCT AND AFFAIRS

OF

NATIONS AND SOVEREIGNS.

By M. DE VATTEL.

A WORK tending to Display the TRUE INTEREST of POWERS.

TRANSLATED from the FRENCH.

VOL. I.

LONDON:

MDCCLX.

As I began reading Vattel's work, I was struck by how closely many of its principles parallel those later articulated in America's founding documents. Concepts such as rights derived from nature, rather than government, appear repeatedly throughout the text. The Declaration of Independence's assertion that rights are "endowed by [our] Creator" and are "unalienable" reflects this natural-law framework.

Additional principles commonly associated with the founding, life, liberty, and the pursuit of happiness; protections against deprivation of life, liberty, or property without due process of law; and freedoms of speech, religion, and the press, are all grounded in long-standing natural law traditions. Even the principle of habeas

38 Emer de Vattel, *The Law of Nations* (1758), title page (edition specifics to be included: publisher/place).

corpus, guaranteeing that no person may be detained except by lawful judgment or the law of the land, predates the American founding and traces as far back as the Magna Carta.

Likewise, the Constitution's Preamble invokes natural law principles through its stated purposes "to establish Justice" and "to secure the Blessings of Liberty." In this sense, the first eight amendments to the Constitution, collectively known as the Bill of Rights, can be understood as positive legal expressions of natural law principles long recognized in Anglo-American legal thought.

This connection became especially clear upon reaching Section 212 of Vattel's *Law of Nations*, which defines the concept of a natural-born citizen. The passage reads:

"The citizens are the members of the civil society; bound to this society by certain duties and subject to its authority, they equally participate in its advantages. The natives, or natural-born citizens, are those born in the country, of parents who are citizens."[39]

The clarity and precision of this definition immediately stood out, echoing principles later embedded in American constitutional discourse and aligning closely with traditional instruction on citizenship that predates the Constitution itself.

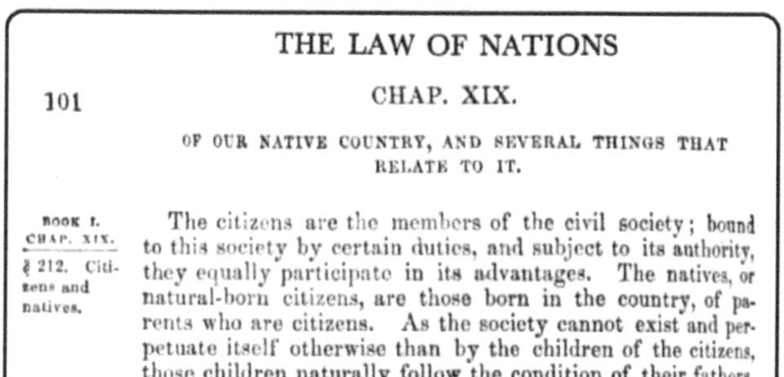
THE LAW OF NATIONS

101 CHAP. XIX.

OF OUR NATIVE COUNTRY, AND SEVERAL THINGS THAT RELATE TO IT.

BOOK I. CHAP. XIX. § 212. Citizens and natives.

The citizens are the members of the civil society; bound to this society by certain duties, and subject to its authority, they equally participate in its advantages. The natives, or natural-born citizens, are those born in the country, of parents who are citizens. As the society cannot exist and perpetuate itself otherwise than by the children of the citizens, those children naturally follow the condition of their fathers, and succeed to all their rights.

Having identified a natural-law definition of a natural-born citizen in Emmerich de Vattel's *Law of Nations*, I continued my research to uncover further connections between natural law and

39 Vattel, *Law of Nations* (1758), bk. I, Ch. 19, § 212.

the Founders' political thought.

In doing so, I came across the 1772 leaflet authored by Samuel Adams, written in the intellectual tradition shaped by James Otis that I referred to earlier. Titled *The Rights of the Colonists,*[40] the pamphlet opens with a section explicitly called "The Natural Rights of the Colonists." From the outset, Adams grounds colonial claims not in parliamentary concession, but in rights derived from God and nature[41]—rights that cannot be surrendered or taken away.

This language closely anticipates the doctrine of "unalienable rights" later articulated in the Declaration of Independence. Throughout the leaflet, Adams repeatedly invokes both "natural law" and "the law of nature," treating them as foundational principles that govern legitimate government.

Adams writes that "just and true liberty, equal and impartial liberty," in matters both spiritual and temporal, is a right to which all men are entitled "by the eternal and immutable laws of God and nature," as well as by "the law of nations, and all well-grounded municipal laws[42], which must have their foundation in the former."

In a second passage, Adams defines natural liberty as freedom from any superior earthly authority, asserting that man ought not be subject to the arbitrary will of another, but instead governed "only to have the law of nature for his rule."[43]

Elsewhere, Adams lists what he calls the core natural rights of the colonists: "First, a right to life; Secondly, to liberty; Thirdly, to property," together with the right to defend those rights. He describes these not as privileges granted by government, but as direct outgrowths of self-preservation, "commonly called the first law of nature." He further insists that all positive and civil laws must conform, as far as possible, "to the law of natural reason and

40 Samuel Adams, The Rights of the Colonists: The Report of the Committee of Correspondence to the Boston Town Meeting, November 20, 1772.

41 Ibid., "Natural Rights of the Colonists" section.

42 Ibid., references to eternal laws of God and nature.

43 https://billofrightsinstitute.org/primary-sources/the-rights-of-the-colonists/

equity."[44]

The Rights of the Colonists provides clear evidence that natural law was not an abstract philosophical influence, but an explicit and operative framework through which colonial leaders articulated rights, liberty, and the legitimate limits of government well before independence.

In the same pamphlet, Adams further explains that natural liberty is not surrendered upon entering civil society but only restrained to the extent necessary for the common good. He emphasizes that individuals consent to society in order to obtain impartial judges and the rule of law, not to abandon their natural rights. Government, in this view, exists to secure justice through law and constitutional order, reinforcing the natural-law principle that civil authority derives from consent and is limited by the very rights it is meant to protect.

Another significant Founder influenced by Emmerich de Vattel's *Law of Nations* was Alexander Hamilton. Born in the British West Indies, Hamilton was sponsored by his employer to travel to North America in 1772 for his education. In 1774, he enrolled in King's College, later renamed Columbia University, where he studied subjects related to national law. During this period, Vattel's *Law of Nations* was commonly used as a foundational text in the study of international and natural law.[45]

Events soon overtook Hamilton's academic pursuits. With the outbreak of the Revolutionary War, he joined the Continental Army, eventually serving as a captain of artillery and later as an aide-de-camp to George Washington.

At roughly the same time, Thomas Jefferson authored a pamphlet entitled *A Summary View of the Rights of British America*. Written in 1774, the document presented what Jefferson described as the "united complaints of his majesty's subjects in America." It was a

44 Ibid.

45 Ron Chernow, Alexander Hamilton (Penguin, 2004), education at King's College.

forceful articulation of colonial grievances, explicitly grounded in natural law.[46]

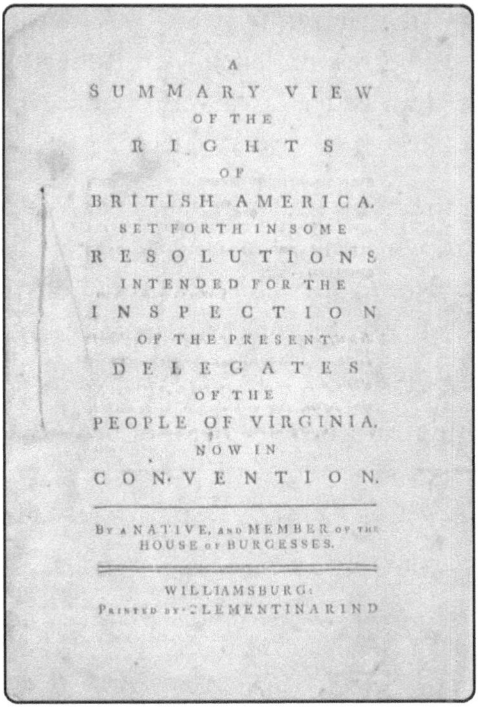

A
SUMMARY VIEW
OF THE
RIGHTS
OF
BRITISH AMERICA.
SET FORTH IN SOME
RESOLUTIONS
INTENDED FOR THE
INSPECTION
OF THE PRESENT
DELEGATES
OF THE
PEOPLE OF VIRGINIA.
NOW IN
CONVENTION.

BY A NATIVE, AND MEMBER OF THE HOUSE OF BURGESSES.

WILLIAMSBURG:
PRINTED BY CLEMENTINA RIND

Jefferson concluded the pamphlet by asserting that the rights claimed by the colonists were not privileges granted by government, but inherent rights derived from nature itself.[47] He wrote:

"That these are our grievances which we have thus laid before his majesty, with that freedom of language and sentiment which becomes a free people claiming their rights, as derived from the laws of nature, and not as the gift of their chief magistrate... but would ill beseem those who are asserting the rights of human nature."

This passage unmistakably reflects the same natural-law framework found in Vattel's *Law of Nations*. It anticipates the principles Jefferson would later articulate in the Declaration of Independence, where rights are again described as inherent,

46 Thomas Jefferson, *A Summary View of the Rights of British America* (July 30, 1774).
47 Ibid.

universal, and not contingent upon governmental grant.

Additional confirmation of Vattel's influence among the Founders appears in a letter written by George Washington on October 6, 1773. In correspondence with Robert Cary & Company, Washington placed an order for several books, including *The Law of Nations*.[48]

Significantly, the book was purchased for Washington's stepson, John Parke Custis, who was preparing to depart for legal studies at King's College in New York. This detail demonstrates that Vattel's work was not merely owned for casual reading but was regarded as an appropriate and necessary text for formal legal education.

George Washington Letter - October 6, 1773

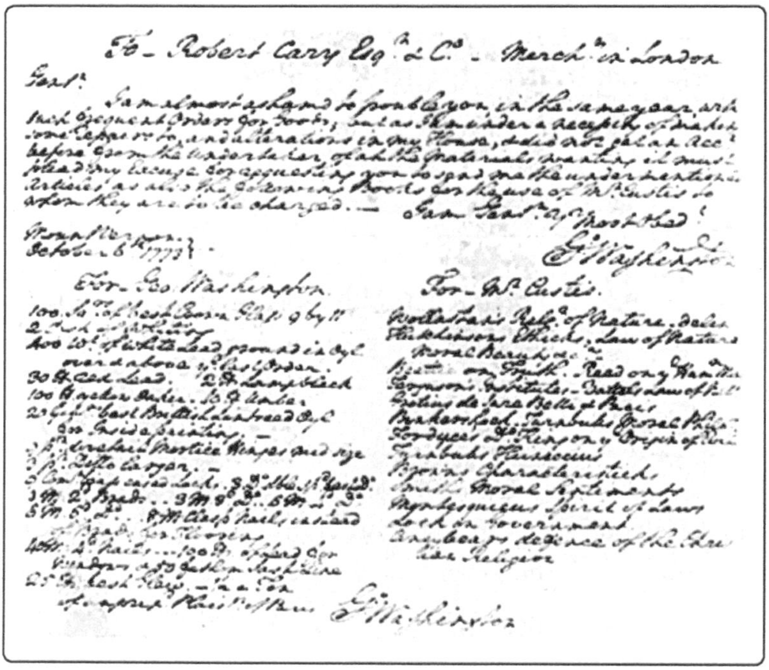

The handwritten invoice accompanying the letter explicitly lists "Vattel's Law of Nature" among the requested titles, alongside works on ethics, moral philosophy, and natural religion.[49] Its inclusion in

48 George Washington to Robert Cary & Co., Oct. 6, 1773, https://founders.archives.gov/documents/Washington/02-09-02-0268

49 "George Washington to Robert Cary & Company, 6 October 1773,"

this list underscores the extent to which natural law, and Vattel's articulation of it, was considered foundational to understanding law, governance, and civic responsibility.

This primary source provides direct evidence that, on the eve of the American Revolution, Vattel's *Law of Nations* was deliberately acquired, studied, and transmitted within the households of the Founders themselves, reinforcing its role as a formative influence on the generation that would soon draft America's founding documents.

In 1774, John Adams reflected on the language and principles adopted by the Continental Congress, explicitly grounding American claims in the immutable laws of nature.[50] Writing later in what would become *The Works of John Adams*, Volume 6, Adams recalled the moment when Congress articulated the foundations of American resistance.

Addressing the American people, Adams wrote:

"Americans! In your Congress at Philadelphia, on Friday, the fourteenth day of October 1774, you laid down the fundamental principles for which you were about to contend, and from which it is to be hoped you will never depart. For asserting and vindicating your rights and liberties, you declared, 'That, by the immutable laws of nature, the principles of the English constitution and your several charters or compacts, you were entitled to life, liberty, and property."[51]

This passage is significant because it reflects not merely personal philosophy, but the collective understanding of the Continental Congress. Rights are described as flowing first from the "immutable laws of nature," with constitutional and chartered protections presented as secondary affirmations rather than original sources.

Founders Online, National Archives, https://founders.archives.gov/documents/Washington/02-09-02-0268 [Original source: The Papers of George Washington, Colonial Series, vol. 9, 8 January 1772–18 March 1774, ed. W. W. Abbot and Dorothy Twohig. Charlottesville: University Press of Virginia, 1994, pp. 343–345.]

50 John Adams, Works of John Adams, Vol. 6.

51 Ibid.

The intellectual continuity here is notable. Samuel Adams and John Adams were cousins, and both were mentored by James Otis, whose natural-law arguments shaped the ideological framework of Massachusetts resistance. Collectively, their writings and actions demonstrate a shared understanding that liberty and property were natural rights, preexisting government and limiting its authority.

By 1774, this natural-law framework was no longer confined to pamphlets or private diaries; it had become the articulated foundation of American political action.

Further evidence that natural law formed a shared and explicit foundation of American political thought appears in the Fairfax Resolves. Drafted on July 18, 1774, at Mount Vernon, the resolves were authored primarily by George Washington and George Mason, and adopted by the freeholders of Fairfax County, Virginia.

The Fairfax Resolves articulated colonial grievances and principles in anticipation of broader intercolonial action. In doing so, they grounded American rights not merely in British custom or royal charter, but in universal principles of natural law and the law of nations.[52]

The meeting minutes record:

"That our Ancestors, when they left their native Land, and settled in America, brought with them (even if Charters had not confirmed the same) the Civil-Constitution and Form of Government of the Country they came from; and were by the Laws of Nature and Nations, entitled to all its Privileges, Immunities and Advantages."[53]

This passage is significant because it explicitly asserts that colonial rights pre-existed written charters and were carried to America by virtue of natural law.[54] Legal rights are thus framed as inherent and portable, grounded in the laws of nature and nations rather than contingent grants from the Crown.

52 "Fairfax County Resolves, 18 July 1774 The Papers of George Washington, Colonial Series, vol. 10 Charlottesville: University Press of Virginia, 1995, pp. 119

53 Ibid.

54 Ibid.

By mid-1774, this language was no longer confined to individual pamphlets or private correspondence. It had become part of formal political resolutions adopted collectively by colonial leaders—further demonstrating that natural law served as a common, organizing principle of American resistance and self-government.

When the First Continental Congress convened in late 1774, the reliance on natural law had evolved from individual arguments into a formal, unified stance. In the resulting Declaration and Resolves, the delegates unanimously grounded American rights in the 'immutable laws of nature.' This was a pivotal moment; it established a shared constitutional vocabulary across twelve colonies, providing the direct intellectual blueprint for the Declaration of Independence two years later.

The resulting document, titled the *Declaration and Resolves of the First Continental Congress*,[55] articulated colonial grievances and asserted the legal and moral foundations of American rights. In doing so, it explicitly grounded those rights in natural law.

The declaration opens with the assertion:

"That the inhabitants of the English colonies in North America, by the immutable laws of nature, the principles of the English constitution, and the several charters or compacts, have the following rights."

55 First Continental Congress, Declaration and Resolves, October 14, 1774. https://www.masshist.org/database/viewer.php?item_id=664&pid=2

[3]

THE good people of the ſeveral colonies of New-Hampſhire, Maſſachuſetts-Bay, Rhode-Iſland and Providence plantations, Connecticut, New-York, New-Jerſey, Pennſylvania, New-Caſtle Kent and Suſſex on Delaware, Maryland, Virginia, North-Carolina, and South-Carolina, juſtly alarmed at theſe arbitrary proceedings of parliament and adminiſtration, have ſeverally elected, conſtituted, and appointed deputies to meet and ſit in general congreſs in the city of Philadelphia, in order to obtain ſuch eſtabliſhment, as that their religion, laws, and liberties may not be ſubverted: Whereupon the deputies ſo appointed being now aſſembled, in a full and free repreſentation of theſe colonies, taking into their moſt ſerious conſideration the beſt means of attaining the ends aforeſaid, do in the firſt place, as Engliſhmen their anceſtors in like caſes have uſually done, for aſſerting and vindicating their rights and liberties, DECLARE,

THAT the inhabitants of the Engliſh colonies in North-America, by the immutable laws of nature, the principles of the Engliſh conſtitution, and the ſeveral charters or compacts, have the following RIGHTS.——

What follows is a detailed enumeration of those rights. Congress affirmed that the colonies were entitled to life, liberty, and property; that these rights had never been surrendered to any foreign power; and that emigration to America did not forfeit the rights of English subjects but carried them intact across the Atlantic.

The resolves further asserted foundational principles of free government, including the right of the people to participate in their legislative councils, the guarantee of trial by jury, the protection of assembly and petition, and the illegality of standing armies maintained without legislative consent.

Significantly, this declaration was not the work of a single author or colony. It was debated, adopted, and agreed to by all delegates present. By October 1774, natural law, described explicitly as the "immutable laws of nature," had become the shared constitutional vocabulary of the American colonies.[56]

The Declaration and Resolves of the First Continental Congress thus stand as a direct antecedent to the Declaration of Independence. Far from inventing a new philosophy in 1776, the Founders formalized a natural-law framework that had already been articulated, debated, and unanimously affirmed in Congress two years earlier.

One week after adopting the Declaration and Resolves of the First Continental Congress, Congress approved the Articles of Association on October 20, 1774, formally committing the colonies to a unified boycott of British goods and signaling an emerging pursuit of economic independence.

In May 1775, Thomas Jefferson was selected as a delegate to the Second Continental Congress. During this period, Jefferson worked closely with Benjamin Franklin, and the two developed a close friendship. Both men were outspoken advocates of resistance to British authority and shared a deep commitment to human rights, grounded in natural law and the law of nations.

Compelling documentary evidence of Vattel's influence within Congress appears in that letter written by Franklin in December 1775 to Charles Guillaume Frédéric Dumas, the editor of the influential edition of *The Law of Nations*. The letter, preserved in congressional and archival records, thanks Dumas for sending three copies of Vattel's work to America.

Franklin wrote:

"I am much obliged by the kind present you have made us of your edition of Vattel. It came to us in good season, when the circumstances of a rising state make it necessary frequently to consult the law of nations. Accordingly, that copy which I kept... has been continually in the hands of the members of our congress,

---

56 Ibid.

now sitting, who are much pleased with your notes and preface, and have entertained a high and just esteem for their author."[57]

Franklin further noted that one copy had been deposited in a public library, another sent to the College of Massachusetts Bay, and the third retained for congressional use. His remarks make clear that Vattel's *Law of Nations* was not merely admired in theory but actively consulted by members of Congress during the critical period in which America was asserting itself as a new and independent political entity.[58]

> BENJAMIN FRANKLIN TO CHARLES-GUILLAUME-FRÉDÉRIC DUMAS, 9 DECEMBER 1775
>
> **To Charles-Guillaume-Frédéric Dumas**
>
> Reprinted from *The Port Folio*, II (1802), 236–7; extracts: American Philosophical Society; Archives du Ministère des affaires étrangères, Paris; Algemeen Rijksarchief, the Hague. 1
>
> DEAR SIR, Philadelphia December 9, 1775.
>
> I received your several favours, of May 18, June 30, and July 8, by Messrs. Vaillant and Pochard; 2 whom, if I could serve upon your recommendation, it would give me great pleasure. Their total want of English is at present an obstruction to their getting any employment among us; but I hope they will soon obtain some knowledge of it. This is a good country for artificers or farmers, but gentlemen, of mere science in *les belles lettres*, cannot so easily subsist here, there being little demand for their assistance among an industrious people, who, as yet, have not much leisure for studies of that kind.
>
> I am much obliged by the kind present you have made us of your edition of Vattel. It came to us in good season, when the circumstances of a rising state make it necessary frequently to consult the law of nations. Accordingly, that copy which I kept, (after depositing one in our own public library here, and sending the other to the college of Massachusetts Bay, as you directed 3) has been continually in the hands of the members of our congress, now sitting, who are much pleased with your notes and preface, and have entertained a high and just esteem for their author. Your

When considered alongside earlier evidence of circulation, education, and citation, Franklin's letter demonstrates that Vattel's *Law of Nations* functioned as a practical reference for the Continental Congress at the very moment the colonies were transitioning from resistance to self-governance.

57 Benjamin Franklin to Charles Dumas, 9 December 1775 https://founders.archives.gov/documents/Franklin/01-22-02-0172

58 Ibid.

Several years before Benjamin Franklin's December 1775 letter thanking Dumas for copies of *The Law of Nations*, the two men had already become acquainted. While traveling through Holland on his way to France near the beginning of the American Revolution, Franklin met Dumas. He quickly recognized his intellectual abilities, commitment to liberty, and enthusiasm for the American cause.

Dumas, a native of Switzerland who spent much of his life in Holland, was a scholar of the ancient classics and several modern languages. Around 1770, he published an influential edition of Vattel's *Law of Nations*, complete with an extensive preface and annotations reflecting his liberal political views. His work placed him at the intersection of natural law theory and emerging revolutionary politics.

Recognizing these qualifications, Franklin recommended Dumas for service to the American cause. When Congress established the Committee of Secret Correspondence in late 1775, with Franklin serving as its chairman, Dumas was appointed as a secret agent representing American interests in Holland.[59]

Acting initially in a covert capacity, Dumas maintained a continuous correspondence with Congress throughout the Revolution. He later served as secretary and translator to John Adams during Adams's diplomatic mission to the Netherlands, and afterward as the United States' chargé d'affaires. In that role, Dumas helped facilitate diplomatic recognition and exchanged treaty ratifications with the Dutch government.[60]

Congressional records describe Dumas's service as unremitting and essential, marked by deep devotion to the rights and liberties for which the United States was contending. Despite modest compensation and personal hardship, he remained steadfast in

59 "The Commissioners to C. W. F. Dumas, 10 April 1778," Founders Online, National Archives, https://founders.archives.gov/documents/Adams/06-06-02-0010 [Original source: The Adams Papers, Papers of John Adams, vol. 6, March–August 1778, ed. Robert J. Taylor. Cambridge, MA: Harvard University Press, 1983, pp. 21–22.]

60 Jared Sparks, ed., Diplomatic Correspondence of the American Revolution VOL. IX BOSTON: NATHAN HALE AND GRAY & BOWEN; G. & C. &. H. CARVILL, NEW YORK; P. THOMPSON, WASHINGTON. 1830.

advancing American diplomatic and commercial interests abroad.

In December 1775, the Committee of Secret Correspondence formally tasked Dumas with exploring whether European powers might, "from principles of humanity," be willing to assist an oppressed people or, should the colonies declare independence, enter into alliances for the benefit of commerce. This directive underscores how deeply the emerging United States relied on the law of nations, both as a philosophical framework and as a practical guide, in navigating its transition from colony to sovereign state.

That the editor of Vattel's *Law of Nations* served simultaneously as a trusted agent of the Continental Congress powerfully illustrates the extent to which natural law and the law of nations were not merely referenced by the Founders but actively embedded in the diplomatic and governmental machinery of the American Revolution.[61]

On April 30, 1776, Benjamin Franklin received a reply from Charles Guillaume Frédéric Dumas, formally accepting his role as an agent of the American cause.[62] Responding to the commission issued by the Committee of Secret Correspondence, Dumas wrote:

"I am deeply... honored by...the confidence reposed in me by the committee... I shall... be devoted to the service of so glorious and just a cause. I accept, therefore, joyfully the commission you have bestowed, and whatever you may think fit to give me in future, and I promise a hearty goodwill and an untiring zeal."[63]

This response is significant not only for its tone but for its timing. Written just weeks before the Declaration of Independence, Dumas's letter confirms that the same individual who edited Vattel's *Law of Nations* was actively and willingly engaged in advancing American diplomatic and commercial interests under congressional authority.[64]

---

61 "Benjamin Franklin to Charles-Guillaume-Frédéric Dumas, 9 December 1775," Founders Online, National Archives, https://founders.archives.gov/documents/Franklin/01-22-02-0172.

62 The Diplomatic Correspondence of the American Revolution, Vol. IX by Jared Sparks 1829-30 https://archive.org/details/diplomaticcorres09sparuoft

63 https://allthingsliberty.com/2015/04/charles-dumas-deals-with-the-dutch/

64 Ibid.

His language reflects a shared moral framework grounded in justice, liberty, and natural law rather than mere political convenience.

By April 1776, the principles articulated in the law of nations were no longer theoretical references. They had become operative commitments guiding American diplomacy, alliances, and assertions of sovereignty on the international stage.

On June 12, 1776, less than a month before the Declaration of Independence, the Virginia Declaration of Rights[65] was adopted by the Fifth Virginia Convention at Williamsburg. Drafted principally by George Mason, the declaration articulated a comprehensive statement of natural rights that would profoundly influence both the Declaration of Independence and the Bill of Rights.

From its opening section, the Virginia Declaration grounds political authority in natural law. Section 1 declares:

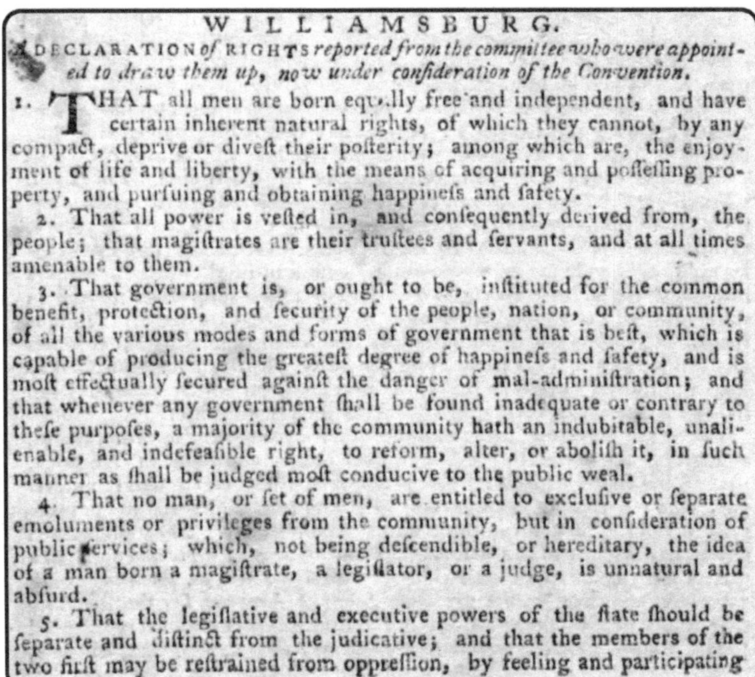

WILLIAMSBURG.

A DECLARATION *of* RIGHTS *reported from the committee who were appointed to draw them up, now under consideration of the Convention.*

1. THAT all men are born equally free and independent, and have certain inherent natural rights, of which they cannot, by any compact, deprive or divest their posterity; among which are, the enjoyment of life and liberty, with the means of acquiring and possessing property, and pursuing and obtaining happiness and safety.

2. That all power is vested in, and consequently derived from, the people; that magistrates are their trustees and servants, and at all times amenable to them.

3. That government is, or ought to be, instituted for the common benefit, protection, and security of the people, nation, or community, of all the various modes and forms of government that is best, which is capable of producing the greatest degree of happiness and safety, and is most effectually secured against the danger of mal-administration; and that whenever any government shall be found inadequate or contrary to these purposes, a majority of the community hath an indubitable, unalienable, and indefeasible right, to reform, alter, or abolish it, in such manner as shall be judged most conducive to the public weal.

4. That no man, or set of men, are entitled to exclusive or separate emoluments or privileges from the community, but in consideration of public services; which, not being descendible, or hereditary, the idea of a man born a magistrate, a legislator, or a judge, is unnatural and absurd.

5. That the legislative and executive powers of the state should be separate and distinct from the judicative; and that the members of the two first may be restrained from oppression, by feeling and participating

65 "The Virginia Declaration of Rights (George Mason's Draft)," Document Bank of Virginia, accessed February 22, 2026, https://www.lva.virginia.gov/collections/educator-resources/dbva/items/show/184

"That all men are born equally free and independent, and have certain inherent natural rights, of which, when they enter into a state of society, they cannot, by any compact, deprive or divest their posterity; of which are, the enjoyment of life and liberty, with the means of acquiring and possessing property, and pursuing and obtaining happiness and safety."

This language is striking for both its clarity and its timing. Rights are described as inherent, natural, and inalienable by compact, directly echoing the natural-law principles long articulated by colonial leaders and theorists of the law of nations. The declaration affirms that civil society exists to secure these rights, not to create or revoke them.

Adopted before independence was formally declared, the Virginia Declaration of Rights demonstrates that natural law had already been translated into binding constitutional language at the state level. It stands as a direct precursor to the national articulation that would follow in July 1776, confirming that the Declaration of Independence did not introduce a novel theory of rights, but gave voice to a framework already embraced and enacted by the American people.

In June of 1776, just six months after Benjamin Franklin wrote that Vattel's *Law of Nations* had been "continually in the hands" of Congress, Franklin and Thomas Jefferson were appointed to the Committee of Five and tasked with drafting a Declaration of Independence.

The Committee of Five consisted of John Adams of Massachusetts, Benjamin Franklin of Pennsylvania, Roger Sherman of Connecticut, Thomas Jefferson of Virginia, and Robert R. Livingston of New York. Each brought to the task a shared grounding in natural-law philosophy and the law of nations.

Jefferson was selected to prepare the initial draft. After review and edits by Franklin and the Committee, the document, titled "A Declaration by the Representatives of the United States of America, in General Congress assembled," was presented to Congress on June 28, 1776.

From its opening paragraph, the Declaration situates American independence within the framework of natural law:

"When in the Course of human events, it becomes necessary for one people to dissolve the political bands which have connected them with another, and to assume among the powers of the earth, the separate and equal station to which the Laws of Nature and of Nature's God[66] entitle them, a decent respect to the opinions of mankind requires that they should declare the causes which impel them to the separation."

This language closely tracks the principles articulated in Vattel's *Law of Nations*, whose full title, *The Law of Nations, or, Principles of the Law of Nature Applied to the Conduct and Affairs of Nations and Sovereigns*, explicitly frames international legitimacy in terms of natural law. Vattel addresses precisely the circumstances described by Jefferson, writing:

"But, when the bands of the political society are broken, or at least suspended, between the sovereign and his people, the contending parties may then be considered as two distinct powers..."[67]

The conceptual parallels are striking. Both texts treat people as moral actors entitled, under the law of nature, to reassume sovereignty and enter the international community as equal powers when political bonds are dissolved.

In July 1776, natural law was formally proclaimed to the world as the foundation of American sovereignty. By internalizing and operationalizing these principles during the Revolution, the Founders set the stage for a new constitutional order, one that would soon require them to codify these very concepts of birth and allegiance into the fixed requirements of the Presidency itself.

---

66 Declaration of Independence (July 4, 1776).

67 Emer de Vattel, *The Law of Nations*; or, Principles of the Law of Nature, bk. II, Ch. IV, §56

II

After Independence: The Early Republic

How the Founders applied natural law in governance, diplomacy, and early legislation

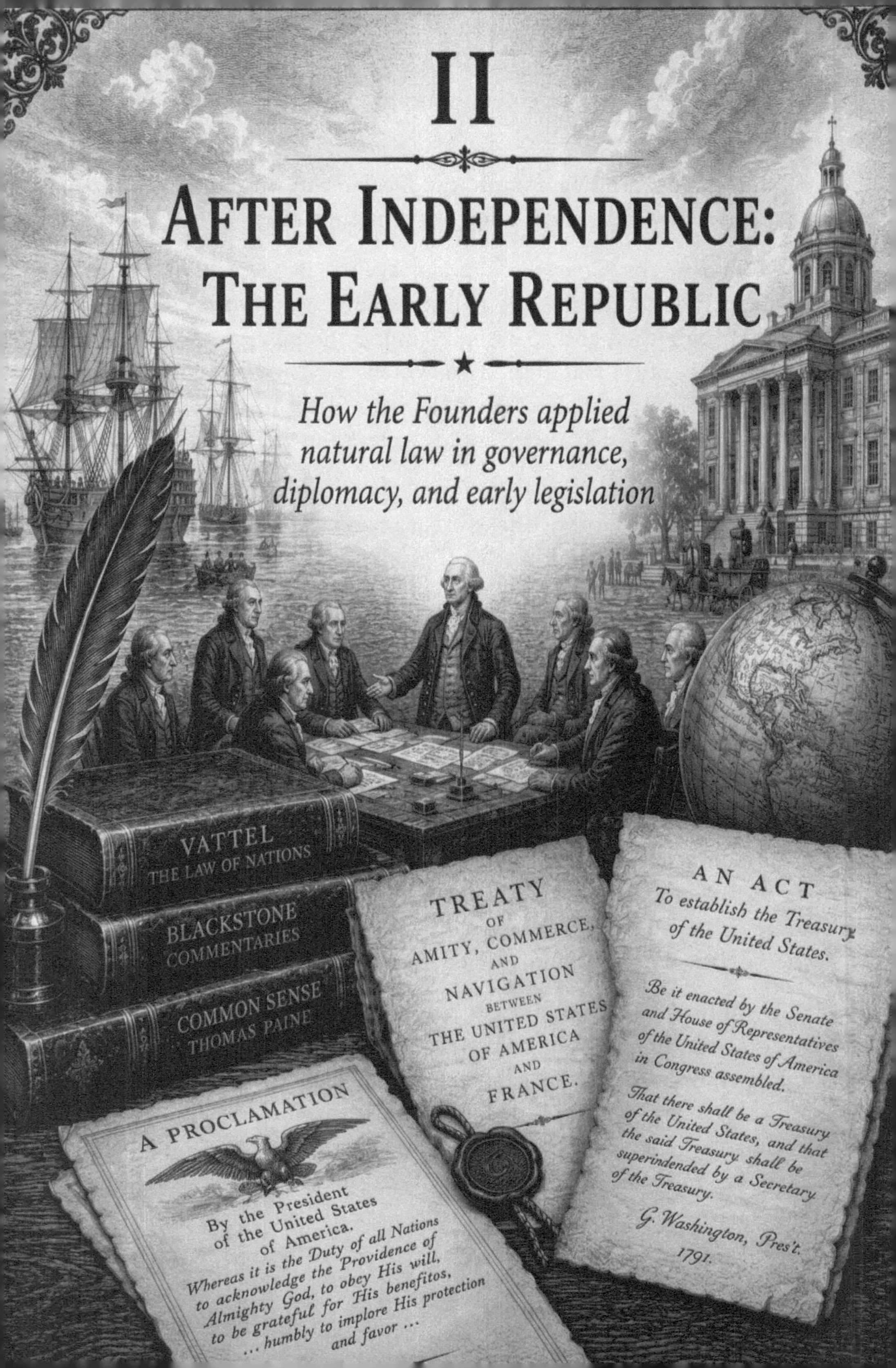

II

After Independence: The Early Republic

How the Founders applied natural law in governance, diplomacy, and early legislation

After the colonies dissolved their political bonds with Great Britain, they entered, as contemporary writers described, a state of nature with respect to external sovereignty. Until a formal national government was established, the former colonies governed themselves according to the law of nature and the law of nations, relying on inherited principles of natural right and consent.

On June 11, 1776, Congress appointed a committee to draft a plan of confederation. More than a year later, on November 15, 1777, the Second Continental Congress adopted the Articles of *Confederation*.[68] Full ratification by all thirteen states was completed on March 1, 1781, at which point the Articles became the operative framework of American government. The United States would remain under this system until the ratification of the Constitution on June 21, 1788.

As mentioned earlier, during the Revolutionary War, Alexander Hamilton was appointed aide-de-camp to George Washington on March 1, 1777, a position he held until February 16, 1781. Following the war, Hamilton resumed formal legal study and gained access to James Duane's extensive law library. In 1782, Hamilton was admitted

68 Articles of Confederation adopted Nov. 15, 1777; ratified Mar. 1, 1781.

to the New York Bar and soon began arguing cases that would shape early American constitutional law.

One such case, *Rutgers v. Waddington* (1784),[69] became a landmark decision for its use of natural law in judicial reasoning. The dispute arose from a conflict between a New York statute and obligations imposed by an international treaty. Hamilton successfully argued that the statute must yield to higher law, grounding his reasoning in the law of nations. In his arguments, Hamilton repeatedly cited *The Law of Nations* and referenced Vattel by name numerous times, demonstrating that natural law continued to function as an operative legal standard after independence.

The Articles of Confederation themselves reflected this natural-law inheritance. They vested the national government with powers essential to sovereign equality among nations, including the authority to declare war, appoint ambassadors, enter treaties, manage alliances, commission military officers, and conduct relations with native nations. These powers mirror the core competencies recognized by the law of nations as attributes of independent states. The articles also presupposed inherent rights, life, liberty, and the pursuit of happiness, understood as natural rights rather than grants of government.

At the state level, natural law likewise continued to guide legislative development. An early example is Thomas Jefferson's Virginia Statute for Religious Freedom.[70] Though initially introduced earlier and initially failing to pass, the statute was adopted word-for-word by the Virginia General Assembly in 1786. Jefferson regarded the measure as a declaration of principle rather than a mere policy choice, and it would later serve as a model for protections incorporated into the Bill of Rights.

In the statute itself, Jefferson explicitly grounded religious liberty in natural law, writing that the rights asserted were "of the

---

69 *Rutgers v. Waddington*, Mayor's Ct. of N.Y.C. (Aug. 27, 1784)

70 Jefferson, Thomas - Virginia statute for religious freedom (enacted January 16, 1786). https://founders.archives.gov/documents/Jefferson/01-02-02-0132-0004-0082

natural rights of mankind,"[71] and that any future act repealing or narrowing them would constitute "an infringement of natural right." This language confirms that, even after independence, American lawmakers continued to understand fundamental liberties as pre-political and binding upon government.

These developments show that the end of colonial rule did not mark a departure from natural law. Rather, the post-Revolutionary period reflects its continued application, in courts, legislatures, and early constitutional structures, as the United States worked to translate principles of natural right into durable institutions of self-government.

Approximately ten years after completing his studies at the College of William & Mary, the college's rector invited Thomas Jefferson to return and assist with major curricular reforms, as well as to contribute to an ambitious architectural redesign of the campus.

Construction on Jefferson's proposed "quadrangle" began in 1774 and was intended to triple the size of the college.[72] The project was abruptly halted in 1775 with the outbreak of the Revolutionary War and was never completed. In 2014, archaeological excavations uncovered the original foundations laid under Jefferson's direction, confirming that the expansion had begun but was interrupted by the conflict.

After American independence, Jefferson returned to William & Mary in a different capacity. Serving as Governor of Virginia and as a member of the college's Board of Visitors, he resumed efforts to reform the institution. In 1779, Jefferson drafted and implemented a sweeping reorganization of the curriculum, as documented in *The William and Mary Quarterly.*

Jefferson's reforms abolished the traditional classical department and the two divinity schools, replacing them with chairs in medicine, law, and modern languages. This marked a decisive shift away from

71 Ibid.
72 https://www.monticello.org/encyclopedia/college-william-and-mary

clerical education toward civic and professional training suited to a republican form of government.

Of particular significance was Jefferson's creation of a new law curriculum titled "Class of National Law."[73] The primary textbook assigned to this course was *The Law of Nations* by Emmerich de Vattel. According to *Early Courses and Professors at William and Mary College* (1905), Vattel's *Law of Nations* was taught at William & Mary earlier than at any other college in the United States.

This development is highly instructive. In the immediate post-Revolutionary period, Jefferson deliberately positioned the law of nations and its natural-law foundations at the center of legal education. The same principles invoked to justify independence and govern diplomacy were now being taught formally to future lawyers, judges, and statesmen, ensuring continuity between revolutionary theory and republican governance.

Institutional records from 1837 provide further proof that this was no passing trend. In the *Laws and Regulations of the College of William and Mary*, the 'Class of National Law' explicitly mandated Vattel's *Law of Nations* as the primary textbook. This indicates that even fifty years after independence, the natural-law framework was being systematically transmitted to the next generation of American public officials.

College of William and Mary 17

TEXT BOOKS

Junior Moral Class — Blair's Lectures, Hedge's Logic, Paley's Moral Philosophy, Manual of History by the Professor.

Junior Mathematical Class — Day's Algebra, Legendre's Geometry, Gummere's Surveying.

Chemical Class — Turner's Chemistry, 5th edition.

Class of National Law — Vattel's Law of Nations.

Senior Political Class — Brown's Lectures, Smith's Wealth of Nations, McCulloch's Outlines of Political Economy.

73 "Early Courses and Professors at William and Mary College." The William and Mary College Quarterly Historical Magazine 14, no. 2 (1905) 76 https://doi.org/10.2307/1916340

This record is significant for two reasons. First, it confirms that Jefferson's 1779 curricular reform, which introduced the Class of National Law, was not a temporary experiment but became a sustained feature of the college's legal instruction.

Second, it demonstrates that Vattel's *Law of Nations* remained the foundational textbook for that course approximately fifty years after independence.

By the early nineteenth century, William & Mary had educated generations of lawyers, legislators, and public officials. The continued use of Vattel in its national law curriculum[74] indicates that the law of nations and its natural-law foundations were not confined to the Revolutionary era but were systematically transmitted to future leaders of the republic.

Jefferson's reforms, together with earlier documentary evidence, reinforce the conclusion that natural law and the law of nations formed a durable component of early American legal education and constitutional understanding.

Thomas Jefferson was the first apprentice of George Wythe, one of the most respected legal minds of the Revolutionary era. Wythe later taught the first law class instituted under Jefferson's 1779 reforms at the College of William & Mary. Among Wythe's students were John Marshall, who would become the longest-serving Chief Justice in United States history, and Henry Clay, one of the most influential legislators of the early republic. Both Marshall and Clay were formed within a legal tradition steeped in natural law and the law of nations.

As Chief Justice, Marshall would later decide cases implicating questions of sovereignty, citizenship, and international obligation. In several opinions, he referred to the law of nations and, in one instance, cited Vattel by name. These judicial references confirm that Vattel's framework remained part of American constitutional

74 Laws and Regulations of the College of William and Mary, in Virginia*, Vol. XI, no. 2 (October 1917) (Williamsburg, VA: College of William and Mary, 1837), 17 https://books.google.com/books?id=C4kfAAAAYAAJ&pg=PA17

reasoning into the early nineteenth century. (These cases will be examined in detail in a later chapter.)

Meanwhile, on the diplomatic front, the influence of the law of nations was equally evident. In 1782, John Adams was appointed the first United States minister to the Netherlands. Working alongside Ben Franklin and John Jay, Adams relied upon Charles Guillaume Frédéric Dumas, formerly the secret agent and editor of Vattel's *Law of Nations*, to serve as secretary and translator.

Dumas played a meaningful role in facilitating American diplomatic efforts, including negotiations connected to the 1778 Treaty of Alliance with France, the 1782 Treaty with the Dutch Republic, the 1783 Treaty of Paris, and subsequent treaties such as the 1783 Treaty with Sweden and the 1785 Treaty of Amity and Commerce with Prussia. These agreements were negotiated within the established framework of the law of nations, the recognized body of international legal principles governing sovereign states.

Further evidence of this framework appears in Jonathan Elliot's *The American Diplomatic Code*,[75] a collection of treaties and conventions between the United States and foreign powers from 1778 to 1834. The volume includes discussions of judicial decisions related to foreign relations and identifies the law of nations as the governing legal standard in matters of diplomacy.

---

75 Elliot, Jonathan. The American Diplomatic Code, Embracing a Collection of Treaties and Conventions Between the United States and Foreign Powers. New York: B. Franklin, 1834.

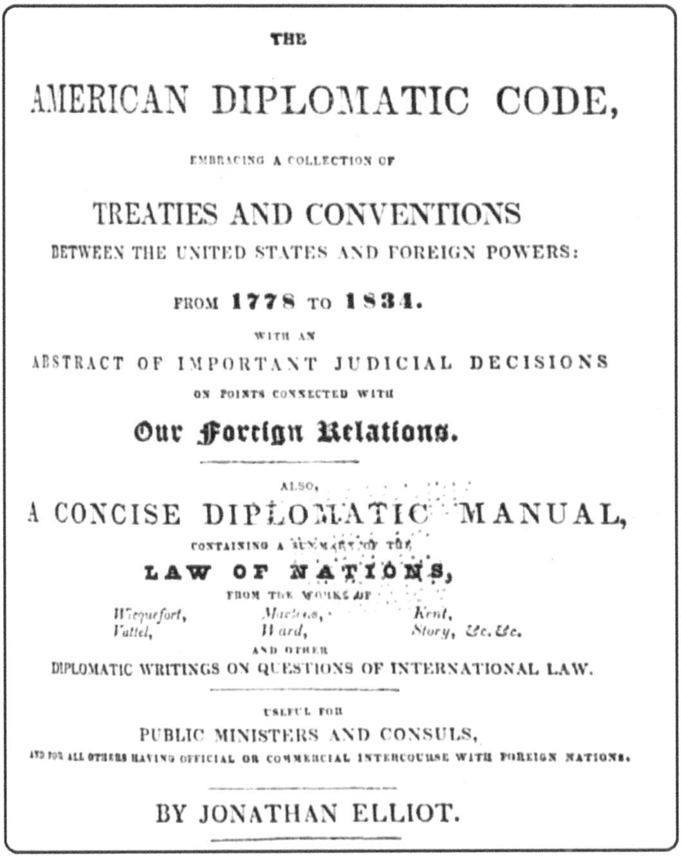

THE

AMERICAN DIPLOMATIC CODE,

EMBRACING A COLLECTION OF

TREATIES AND CONVENTIONS

BETWEEN THE UNITED STATES AND FOREIGN POWERS:

FROM 1778 TO 1834.

WITH AN

ABSTRACT OF IMPORTANT JUDICIAL DECISIONS

ON POINTS CONNECTED WITH

Our Foreign Relations.

ALSO,

A CONCISE DIPLOMATIC MANUAL,

CONTAINING A SUMMARY OF THE

LAW OF NATIONS,

FROM THE WORKS OF

Wicquefort, *Martens*, *Kent*,
Vattel, *Ward*, *Story*, &c. &c.

AND OTHER

DIPLOMATIC WRITINGS ON QUESTIONS OF INTERNATIONAL LAW.

USEFUL FOR

PUBLIC MINISTERS AND CONSULS,

AND FOR ALL OTHERS HAVING OFFICIAL OR COMMERCIAL INTERCOURSE WITH FOREIGN NATIONS.

BY JONATHAN ELLIOT.

Within this compilation, the term "the law of nations" appears repeatedly, and Vattel is cited among the authorities shaping diplomatic understanding. This recurring reference demonstrates that American treaty-making and foreign policy were conducted within a recognized natural-law and law-of-nations framework, consistent with the intellectual foundations laid during the Revolutionary era.

The cumulative record, educational, judicial, and diplomatic, reveals that the early United States did not abandon natural law after independence. Instead, it operationalized those principles in treaty negotiation, judicial interpretation, and constitutional development. *The law of nations* functioned not merely as rhetoric, but as a practical guide in securing recognition and equality among the powers of the earth.

If you have followed the evidence presented thus far, it should be clear that natural law and the law of nations formed a shared intellectual foundation among the principal architects of the American Republic. Figures such as George Mason, John Jay, John Adams, George Washington, Benjamin Franklin, Thomas Jefferson, Samuel Adams, Alexander Hamilton, George Wythe, John Marshall, and James Otis demonstrably engaged with natural-law reasoning and, in many documented instances, with Emmerich de Vattel's *Law of Nations* specifically.

The cumulative record shows that Vattel's work circulated widely among the Founding generation, was taught in early American law curricula, was cited in judicial opinions, was consulted in Congress, and was relied upon in diplomatic negotiations. It was not an obscure European treatise; it was a recognized authority on sovereignty, allegiance, and the rights and duties of nations.

Among the subjects addressed in Vattel's work is Section 212 of Book I, which defines "citizens and natives," including the concept of a "natural-born citizen."[76] Given the documented presence of Vattel's treatise in the intellectual and institutional life of the Founding era, it is highly significant that Article II of the Constitution would later restrict eligibility for the presidency to a "natural-born Citizen."

Whether by direct reading, formal legal instruction, or immersion in the prevailing law-of-nations framework, the framers operated within a shared understanding of sovereignty, allegiance, and political membership that drew from the same natural-law tradition Vattel articulated. The term "natural-born Citizen" did not appear in a vacuum; it emerged from an established legal vocabulary familiar to the generation that drafted and ratified the Constitution.

Before proceeding further, it is necessary to examine the presidential eligibility clause itself. Article II, Section 1 of the Constitution provides:

---

76 Emer de Vattel, *The Law of Nations* (1758), Book I, §212.

"No Person except a natural-born Citizen, or a Citizen of the United States, at the time of the Adoption of this Constitution, shall be eligible to the Office of President; neither shall any Person be eligible to that Office who shall not have attained to the Age of thirty five Years, and been fourteen Years a Resident within the United States."[77]

The clause distinguishes between two categories:

(1) a "natural-born Citizen," and

(2) a "Citizen of the United States, at the time of the Adoption of this Constitution."

The second category was plainly transitional. It ensured that members of the founding generation, who had been born British subjects but became American citizens upon independence, would not be excluded from eligibility. Today, that category has no practical application. The operative constitutional requirement is that the President must be a "natural-born Citizen."

The presence of two separate categories raises a critical interpretive question: What did the framers mean by "natural-born Citizen"?

As shown in earlier chapters, the Founding generation operated within a legal vocabulary deeply influenced by natural law and the law of nations. In that framework, citizenship was tied not merely to territory, but to allegiance and political membership. Vattel's *Law of Nations* defined "natural-born citizens" as those born in the country to citizen parents, a definition situated within a broader theory of sovereignty and inherited political allegiance.

If that understanding informed the framers' thinking, then the inclusion of a transitional "Citizen at the time of the Adoption" clause makes structural sense. The framers themselves had not been born citizens of an independent United States; they became citizens through the act of independence. The temporary provision ensured

77 U.S. Const. art. II, § 1, cl. 5.

that revolutionary leaders such as George Washington, John Adams, and others were eligible to serve, while preserving a stricter standard for future generations.

Early drafts of the Constitution reflect similar thinking. In a June 18, 1787, draft attributed to Alexander Hamilton,[78] Article IX provided that:

"No person shall be eligible to the office of President of the United States unless he be now a Citizen of one of the States, or hereafter be born a Citizen of the United States."

The evolution of this clause demonstrates that the framers deliberately distinguished between existing citizens and those who would be "natural-born." The constitutional question, therefore, is not whether a distinction exists; it plainly does, but what legal meaning the framers attached to the term "natural-born Citizen" within their established natural-law framework.

During the Constitutional Convention of 1787, multiple plans were proposed and debated, including the Virginia Plan (introduced by Edmund Randolph but largely drafted by James Madison) and alternative proposals that were later reconciled through compromise.

The final language of the Constitution emerged from the Committee of Style and Arrangement, whose members included Alexander Hamilton, William Samuel Johnson, Rufus King, James Madison, and Gouverneur Morris. The committee transformed twenty-three previously approved resolutions into the final draft presented on September 17, 1787.[79]

Earlier drafts of Article II referred simply to a "citizen." However, during the Convention, the qualification was revised to require that the President be a "natural-born Citizen."

78 "Draft of a Constitution, [17 September 1787]," Founders Online, National Archives, https://founders.archives.gov/documents/Hamilton/01-04-02-0137 [Original source: The Papers of Alexander Hamilton, vol. 4, January 1787–May 1788, ed. Harold C. Syrett. New York: Columbia University Press, 1962, pp. 253–274.]

79 Max Farrand, ed., The Records of the Federal Convention of 1787 (New Haven: Yale University Press, 1911).

The pivot from a general 'citizen' requirement to the specific 'natural-born' qualification is often traced to a single, urgent hint from John Jay. Writing to George Washington in July 1787, Jay expressed a profound concern regarding foreign influence, suggesting a 'strong check' by requiring the Commander-in-Chief to be a 'natural-born Citizen.' Jay's original letter, with the word *born* italicized for emphasis, signaled that the place of birth was secondary to a condition of birth, one defined by undivided allegiance.

> LXVIII. John Jay to George Washington.[3]
>
> New York 25 July 1787
>
> Permit me to hint, whether it would not be wise & seasonable to provide a a strong check to the admission of Foreigners into the administration of our national Government; and to declare expresly that the Command in chief of the american army shall not be given to, nor devolve on, any but a natural *born* Citizen.

On September 2, 1787, Washington replied briefly, stating:

"I thank you for the hints contained in your letter."[80]

> XCIX. George Washington to John Jay.[2]
>
> Philadelphia Sept. 2d 1787
>
> I regret not having had it in my power to visit New York during the adjournment of the Convention, last Month. — not foreseeing with any precission the period at which it was likely to take place or the length of it, I had put my carriage in the hands of a workman to be repaired and had not the means of mooving during the recess but with, or the curtisy of, others.
>
> I thank you for the hints contained in your letter

The effect of Jay's suggestion was immediate. On September 4, 1787, as recorded in Madison's notes of the Federal Convention, the revised language appeared in the Committee's report. What had previously been a generic qualification was now narrowed, reflecting the delegates' consensus that birth-based allegiance was necessary for the executive office.

---

80 "George Washington to John Jay, 2 September 1787," Founders Online, National Archives, https://founders.archives.gov/documents/Washington/04-05-02-0282 [Original source: The Papers of George Washington, Confederation Series, vol. 5, 1 February 1787–31 December 1787, ed. W. W. Abbot. Charlottesville: University Press of Virginia, 1997, pp. 307–308.]

> 498 RECORDS OF THE FEDERAL CONVENTION
>
> *Tuesday* MADISON *September 4*
>
> (5) 'Sect. 2. No person except a natural born citizen or a Citizen of the U— S— at the time of the adoption of this Constitution shall be eligible to the office of President; nor shall any person be elected to that office, who shall be under the age of thirty five years, and who has not been in the whole, at least fourteen years a resident within the U— S.'

While the Convention records do not preserve extended debate on this specific wording change, the chronological proximity between Jay's recommendation and the Committee's adoption of the revised qualification is notable. At a minimum, the correspondence demonstrates that concerns about foreign influence and allegiance were actively circulating among leading figures during the final stages of drafting.

The completed Constitution, including the "natural-born Citizen" requirement, was signed on September 17, 1787, and submitted to the states for ratification.

By the time the Constitution was ratified, the phrase "natural-born Citizen" had emerged within a legal culture steeped in natural law, the law of nations, and longstanding concerns regarding allegiance at birth. The historical record demonstrates that the framers' language reflected not an innovation, but a continuation of established principles that had guided American political thought from the Revolution through the Convention.

III

Interpreting Natural Born Citizenship

Debates in Congress, courts, and statutes over the meaning of birth and allegiance

III

Interpreting Natural-born Citizenship

Debates in Congress, courts, and statutes over the meaning of birth and allegiance

In examining the meaning of citizenship and the term "natural-born citizen," this work distinguishes between natural law principles recognized by the Founders, the legislative intent reflected in congressional enactments, especially those of the Reconstruction era, and the judicial interpretations that developed in later periods. Because constitutional language emerged within a framework shaped by the law of nations and by longstanding concepts of allegiance, understanding these historical foundations is essential. This study, therefore, proceeds chronologically, allowing the reader to see how definitions of citizenship were articulated at each stage and to evaluate whether later doctrines remain consistent with those earlier understandings.

After the Constitution was signed on September 17, 1787, it was submitted to the states for ratification. Immediately, critics writing under the pseudonyms "Cato" and "Brutus" began publishing essays opposing the proposed Constitution. These writings would later be grouped under the label *Anti-Federalist Papers*.[81]

In response, Alexander Hamilton began publishing essays in

81 https://history.nycourts.gov/about_period/antifederalist-papers/

defense of the Constitution in October 1787. He soon recruited James Madison and John Jay, and together they produced what would later be known as *The Federalist*, later referred to as *The Federalist Papers*.[82]

Throughout these essays, the framers repeatedly invoked the law of nations and natural law as foundational to constitutional structure.

In *Federalist* No. 3, Jay explains that violations of treaties and the law of nations are just causes of war:

"So far, therefore, as either designed or accidental violations of treaties and the law of nations afford JUST causes of war..."[83]

In *Federalist* No. 42, Madison emphasizes Congress's Article I, Section 8 power:

"The power to define and punish piracies and felonies committed on the high seas and offenses against the law of nations..."[84]

He explains that under the Articles of Confederation, there was no adequate mechanism to address offenses against the law of nations, leaving the Confederacy vulnerable to foreign entanglement.

In *Federalist* No. 43, Madison appeals explicitly to natural law in defending the supersession of the Articles of Confederation:

"...to the transcendent law of nature and of nature's God, which declares that the safety and happiness of society are the objects at which all political institutions aim..."[85]

In *Federalist* No. 53, Madison further notes that federal representatives must be acquainted with treaties, foreign commercial policy, and the law of nations since these matters are entrusted to

82 https://avalon.law.yale.edu/subject_menus/fed.asp

83 John Jay, Federalist No. 3, *in The Federalist Papers*, ed. Clinton Rossiter (New York: Signet Classics, 2003).

84 James Madison, Federalist No. 42, in *The Federalist Papers*, ed. Clinton Rossiter (New York: Signet Classics, 2003).

85 James Madison, Federalist No. 43, in *The Federalist Papers*, ed. Clinton Rossiter (New York: Signet Classics, 2003).

the federal government.[86]

Jay reiterates the supremacy of the law of nations in *Federalist* No. 64, stating that a treaty procured through corruption would be "null and void by the law of nations."[87]

Likewise, in *Federalist* No. 80, Hamilton explains that an unjust sentence against a foreigner could amount to a violation of treaty obligations or the general law of nations.[88]

These repeated references demonstrate that during the ratification debates, the Constitution's defenders continued to frame federal authority, particularly in matters of war, treaties, and foreign relations, within the established principles of natural law and the law of nations.

On June 21, 1788, after nine states had ratified, the Constitution met the threshold required for adoption. By 1789, it was fully in operation as the supreme law of the land.

On April 30, 1789, George Washington was inaugurated as the first President of the United States in New York City. Shortly thereafter, Washington became a patron of the New York Society Library, the city's oldest library.

Library records show that on October 5, 1789, President Washington checked out two volumes. One of them was *The Law of Nations* by Emmerich de Vattel.[89]

In April 2010, the overdue record became the subject of widespread media attention when it was discovered that the books had never been formally returned, resulting in a symbolic fine calculated to be over $300,000.[90] While the monetary figure was

86 James Madison, Federalist No. 53, in *The Federalist Papers*, ed. Clinton Rossiter (New York: Signet Classics, 2003).

87 John Jay, Federalist No. 64, in *The Federalist Papers*, ed. Clinton Rossiter (New York: Signet Classics, 2003).

88 Alexander Hamilton, Federalist No. 80, in *The Federalist Papers*, ed. Clinton Rossiter (New York: Signet Classics, 2003).

89 New York Society Library, borrower ledger entry listing Emer de Vattel, The *Law of Nations*, checked out by George Washington.

90 "George Washington Owes NYC Library $300K for Overdue Books," NBC New

merely a humorous modern calculation, the historical record itself is genuine: Washington borrowed Vattel's *Law of Nations* during the first year of his presidency.

The timing is noteworthy. In 1789, the new federal government was taking shape. The Judiciary Act was enacted, executive departments were being organized, and questions of treaty obligations, foreign recognition, and national sovereignty were immediate concerns. Washington's consultation of Vattel during this period aligns with the broader pattern already documented: the law of nations remained a practical reference point in the early administration of the United States.

Whether for matters of diplomacy, neutrality, or constitutional structure, Vattel's treatise was not confined to the Revolutionary era. It was in the hands of the first President of the United States during the foundational year of the new government.

One of the clearest indicators of how the early Republic understood citizenship is found in the naturalization process itself. The First Congress enacted the Naturalization Act of 1790,[91] establishing the terms under which foreign nationals could become citizens of the United States. However, it was repealed just five years later and replaced with the Naturalization Act of 1795,[92] which was also repealed just three years later.

Although the Naturalization Oath language evolved over time, the core requirement of naturalization required an applicant to renounce prior allegiance and swear fidelity to the United States. Modern codification of that principle appears in Section 337(a) of the Immigration and Nationality Act (8 U.S.C. §1448; 8 CFR 337.1),[93] which requires an applicant to:

- Support the Constitution,

York, April 20, 2010, https://www.nysoclib.org/historic-mount-vernon-returns-copy-rare-book-borrowed-george-washington-1789-new-york-society

91 Naturalization Act of 1790, Ch. 3, 1 Stat. 103 (1790).

92 Naturalization Act of 1795, 1 Stat. 414 (1795).

93 Immigration and Nationality Act § 337(a), 8 U.S.C. § 1448(a); 8 C.F.R. § 337.1.

- Renounce and abjure all allegiance and fidelity to any foreign sovereign,
- Bear true faith and allegiance to the United States,
- And, when required, serve in defense of the nation.

The foundational concept, present from the earliest naturalization statutes, is the transfer of allegiance. Citizenship was not merely residence or presence; it required exclusive political fidelity.

This raises an interpretive question central to the meaning of "natural-born Citizen." If naturalized citizens were required to renounce all foreign allegiance as a condition of entry into American political membership, what did the framers understand about allegiance at birth?

The Founding generation viewed allegiance as a political bond tied to sovereignty. Under the law-of-nations framework widely known at the time, allegiance was not a casual attachment; it was the defining feature of citizenship. The early Congress required naturalizing immigrants to sever prior sovereign ties precisely because divided allegiance was viewed as incompatible with full political membership.

The constitutional structure reinforces this concern. Article II restricts the presidency to a "natural-born Citizen," while permitting existing citizens at the time of adoption to serve. The presidency was uniquely entrusted with command of the armed forces and treaty-making authority, powers deeply intertwined with foreign relations and national security.

Whether the framers intended birth on soil alone to suffice, or birth accompanied by undivided allegiance, is the interpretive question that follows. What is clear is that allegiance, not mere geography, was central to the Founding understanding of political membership.

The Constitution itself embeds the law of nations within its structure.

Article I, Section 8, Clause 10[94] grants Congress the power:

"To define and punish Piracies and Felonies committed on the high Seas, and Offenses against Law of Nations."

This clause recognizes the law of nations as an existing body of law, one whose violations could be defined and punished by Congress. The framers did not invent this law; they assumed its existence and incorporated it into federal authority.

Article VI further elevates international obligations by declaring that treaties made under the authority of the United States "shall be the supreme Law of the Land."[95] This Supremacy Clause confirms that treaties, instruments governed by the law of nations, occupy the highest rank in American law.

The Constitution, therefore, presupposes the continued operation of the law of nations in the new republic. While the document does not name any particular treatise, the historical record shows that Vattel's *Law of Nations* was among the most widely circulated and cited authorities on that subject during the Founding era.

The relevance to Article II becomes clear: if the framers embedded the law of nations into the structure of federal power, into piracy, treaties, and foreign relations, then the use of the term "natural-born Citizen" must also be read within the legal vocabulary familiar to them.

The Constitution does not define the phrase. It assumes its meaning was already understood.

The interpretive question, therefore, is not whether the law of nations was part of the constitutional framework; it plainly was, but whether the Founding generation understood "natural-born Citizen" in light of the same body of law that governed sovereignty, allegiance, and international standing.

94 U.S. Const. art. I, § 8, cl. 10.

95 U.S. Const. art. VI, cl. 2.

The integration of the law of nations into American constitutional practice did not end with ratification. It continued immediately in executive action.

In April 1793, amid the outbreak of war between France and Great Britain, George Washington issued the Neutrality Proclamation.[96] In it, he warned American citizens that violations of neutrality would render them liable to punishment under the law of nations:

"...whosoever of the citizens of the United States shall render himself liable to punishment or forfeiture under the law of nations... will not receive the protection of the United States..."

Washington further directed federal officers to institute prosecutions against those who violated the law of nations with respect to foreign powers at war.

Shortly thereafter, in June 1793, Alexander Hamilton, writing privately to Richard Harison, reinforced the same principle:

"...To do it is an offense against the law of Nations, the law of Nations is a part of the law of the land."[97]

Hamilton's statement is significant. He did not describe the law of nations as advisory, rhetorical, or philosophical. He described it as part of the law of the land, a phrase echoing the Supremacy Clause of Article VI.

These executive and legal affirmations demonstrate that, in practice, the early Republic treated the law of nations as binding domestic law. Violations could trigger prosecution. Citizens were accountable to it. Federal officers were instructed to enforce it.

The same generation that drafted Article II and inserted the phrase "natural-born Citizen" also publicly affirmed that the law of nations formed part of American law. Any interpretation of constitutional terminology must therefore account for the legal

96 George Washington, Proclamation of Neutrality, April 22, 1793, in *The Papers of George Washington, Presidential Series.*

97 Alexander Hamilton to Richard Harison, June 13–15, 1793, Founders Online, National Archives, https://founders.archives.gov/documents/Hamilton/01-14-02-0373

framework that the Founding generation explicitly recognized as operative.

Starting in the eighteenth century and continuing well into the nineteenth, members of Congress repeatedly cited and referenced Vattel by name throughout the Congressional Record. The *Law of Nations* was not treated as obscure philosophy; it was treated as a working authority.

"Twice in the index of the Third Congress (1793), the Senate formally directed the Secretary of State to purchase copies of key legal works for official use.[1] Among those works were Vattel's *Law of Nations.*

On page xiii of the index under "S" for Secretary of State, it asks for "purchase Blackstone's Commentaries and Vattel's *Law of Nations.*"

INDEX—FIRST SESSION, THIRD CONGRESS. xiii

	Page.
Rogers, Jabez, petition of, presented and referred	46
reported on	49
report agreed to	51
Ross, Mr. certificate of his election communicated	60
appeared, qualified, and took his seat	67
Rutherford, Mr. attended	3
leave of absence	33
S.	
Schmyser, Michael, petition of, presented	31
Secretary of Senate to furnish newspapers	7
to purchase Blackstone's Commentaries and Vattel's Laws of Nations	44
to pay John Dunlap for printing journals	80

This directive is significant.

By 1793 — just six years after the Constitutional Convention — the federal government was not merely aware of Vattel's treatise; it was actively acquiring and preserving it as an authoritative legal reference. The same Congress operating under the newly ratified Constitution deemed Vattel's work important enough to procure for official governmental use.

This demonstrates institutional continuity. *The Law of Nations* was not abandoned after independence, nor confined to Revolutionary rhetoric. It remained embedded within the functioning machinery of the federal government.

When Congress ordered the purchase of Vattel's *Law of Nations*, it did so under the authority of the Constitution, the same Constitution that contains the presidential eligibility requirement limiting the office to a "natural-born Citizen."

The interpretive environment in which that clause would operate was therefore one in which Vattel remained an acknowledged and consulted authority.

In addition to the directive found under "S" for Secretary of State, page xiv of that same index provides further confirmation.

"Vattel's Laws of Nations, to be purchased for the use of the Senate."

xiv INDEX—FIRST SESSION, THIRD CONGRESS.

This language is direct and unambiguous. The United States Senate, operating under the newly ratified Constitution, ordered that Vattel's *Law of Nations* be purchased for its official use.

This was not a private acquisition. It was not a passing reference in debate. It was a formal institutional action, recorded in the index of the Third Congress, demonstrating that Vattel's work was considered part of the federal government's legal and diplomatic reference framework.

The same Congress that exercised powers under Article I, including the power "to define and punish Piracies and Felonies committed on the high Seas, and Offenses against the Law of Nations,"[98] ensured that Vattel's treatise was available for its use.

The implication is significant: *The Law of Nations* was not merely a historical influence; it was treated as a contemporary legal authority within the constitutional system itself.

One year later, on March 10, 1794, the Senate again ordered copies of Vattel's *Law of Nations* to be procured for its use.

The *Journal of the Senate* records the following directive:

"Ordered, That the Secretary purchase Blackstone's Commentaries, and Vattel's Law of Nature and Nations, for the use of the Senate."[99]

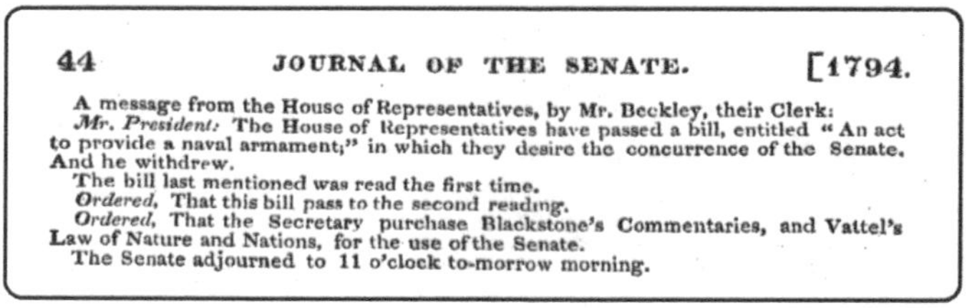

44 JOURNAL OF THE SENATE. [1794.

A message from the House of Representatives, by Mr. Beckley, their Clerk:

Mr. President: The House of Representatives have passed a bill, entitled "An act to provide a naval armament;" in which they desire the concurrence of the Senate. And he withdrew.

The bill last mentioned was read the first time.

Ordered, That this bill pass to the second reading.

Ordered, That the Secretary purchase Blackstone's Commentaries, and Vattel's Law of Nature and Nations, for the use of the Senate.

The Senate adjourned to 11 o'clock to-morrow morning.

This was not a one-time acquisition. It was a deliberate, repeated action.

By 1794, the Senate had now thrice formally ordered Vattel's work for official use. The timing is noteworthy. These orders occurred during the Washington administration, when the Constitution was in its infancy, and the federal government was actively defining its relationship with foreign nations and establishing its constitutional authority.

The Senate, exercising powers expressly granted under Article I, ensured that Vattel's treatise was available as a working reference in matters touching *The Law of Nations*.

98 U.S. Constitution, art. I, § 8, cl. 10.

99 U.S. Senate, index entry under "Vattel's Laws of Nations — to be purchased for the use of the Senate," 3rd Congress (1793–1794).

- The institutional record therefore shows:
- The Founders read and cited Vattel before independence.
- *The Law of Nations* informed Revolutionary and constitutional thought.
- The Constitution expressly recognizes *The Law of Nations.*
- The Executive enforced it.
- The Senate repeatedly formally acquired Vattel's treatise for its official use.

This continuity demonstrates that *The Law of Nations* was not a theoretical background philosophy. It functioned as an operational legal authority within the early constitutional government.[100]

Reliance on Vattel did not end with the early Republic but persisted well into the mid-nineteenth century, long after the Founding generation had passed.

In the official index to the 1843 congressional debates, lawmakers were explicitly directed to consult 'Vattel' for the definition of 'natural allegiance.' This specific terminology, pairing 'natural' with 'allegiance', reinforces the argument that Congress still viewed *The Law of Nations* as the authoritative source for understanding the bond between citizen and sovereign.

By the mid-nineteenth century, nearly sixty years after the Constitutional Convention, Congress still regarded Vattel as an authoritative source on questions of allegiance. The term "natural allegiance" was not left undefined; lawmakers were explicitly directed to Vattel for clarification.

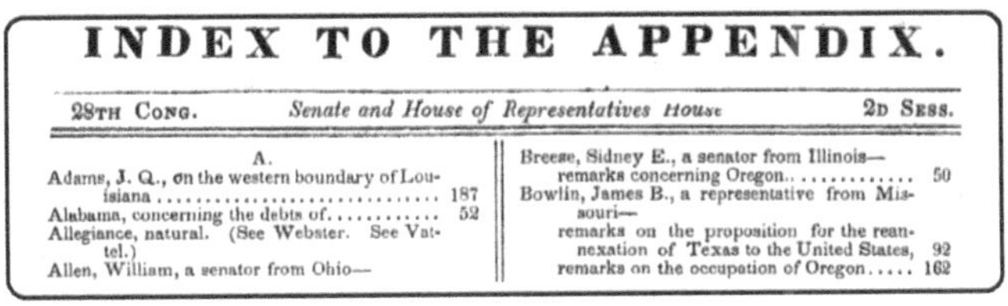

INDEX TO THE APPENDIX.

28TH CONG. *Senate and House of Representatives House* 2D SESS.

A.

Adams, J. Q., on the western boundary of Louisiana 187
Alabama, concerning the debts of........ 52
Allegiance, natural. (See Webster. See Vattel.)
Allen, William, a senator from Ohio—

Breese, Sidney E., a senator from Illinois—
remarks concerning Oregon........ 50
Bowlin, James B., a representative from Missouri—
remarks on the proposition for the reannexation of Texas to the United States, 92
remarks on the occupation of Oregon..... 162

100 See generally U.S. Senate legislative records, 1790s, reflecting acquisition and use of public law treatises including Vattel.

This is not speculative inference. It is an official congressional index instruction.

The pairing is important:

"Allegiance" the political bond between citizen and sovereign.

"Natural" indicates allegiance arising from birth, not by statute.

The fact that Congress cross-referenced Vattel when discussing natural allegiance demonstrates that *The Law of Nations* remained embedded in the legal understanding of citizenship long after ratification.

If legislators in 1843 were instructed to consult Vattel when defining natural allegiance, then any serious interpretation of Article II's "natural-born Citizen" clause must account for that same intellectual framework. While this mid-nineteenth-century precedent underscores the longevity of the law-of-nations framework, understanding its initial application requires a return to the chronological sequence of the early Republic, where these principles were first put to the test on the diplomatic stage.

President George Washington commissioned Chief Justice John Jay to travel to London to negotiate what would become the Treaty of Amity, Commerce, and Navigation with Great Britain, commonly known as the Jay Treaty.[101] The treaty was signed on November 19, 1794, but required Senate ratification before it could take effect.

The treaty proved highly controversial. Opposition was fierce. In response, Alexander Hamilton undertook a public defense of the treaty.

Beginning in August of 1795, Alexander Hamilton published twenty-eight anonymous essays under the pseudonym Camillus, collectively known as *The Defense.*[102] These essays systematically

101 Treaty of Amity, Commerce, and Navigation (Jay Treaty), U.S.-Gr. Brit., Nov. 19, 1794.

102 Alexander Hamilton, "The Defence No. I," July 22, 1795, in Founders Online, National Archives, https://founders.archives.gov/documents/Hamilton/01-18-02-0305-0002

defended both the constitutionality and the necessity of the treaty.

The legal framework Hamilton relied upon throughout these writings is telling.

Across twenty-eight essays:

Vattel is cited by name twenty-nine times.

The term “the law of nations” appears seventy-one times.

Hamilton did not treat *The Law of Nations* as a peripheral theory or rhetorical flourish. He treated it as a binding legal authority, governing treaty obligations, national sovereignty, neutrality, and international conduct.

The Jay Treaty controversy was not abstract. It implicated Article II treaty powers, Article VI supremacy principles, and the constitutional structure of the federal government. Yet in defending the treaty, Hamilton repeatedly grounded his arguments in *The Law of Nations* and in Vattel's treatise.

President Washington formally proclaimed the treaty in effect on February 29, 1796.[103]

The episode demonstrates that, less than a decade after ratification, the Constitution was being interpreted, defended, and operationalized within a legal framework that assumed the authority of *The Law of Nations*. Vattel's treatise was not a historical background; it remained an active guide in matters touching sovereignty, allegiance, and national character.

The continuity of *The Law of Nations* did not remain confined to Congress or the Executive. It also appears in early Supreme Court jurisprudence.

While some judicial statements constitute dicta, language not essential to the holding, such statements may still serve as persuasive

103 "Proclamation Declaring the Jay Treaty in Force." February 29, 1796. In The Papers of George Washington, Presidential Series, vol. 19. https://www.mountvernon.org/library/digitalhistory/digital-encyclopedia/article/neutrality-proclamation

authority. More importantly, when a Justice cites a specific legal authority, it confirms that the work was considered relevant and authoritative in resolving questions before the Court.

In the 1814 case of *The Venus*,[104] Chief Justice John Marshall addressed questions concerning the national character of individuals and vessels during wartime. In a partial concurrence and partial dissent, Marshall grounded his analysis explicitly in *The Law of Nations*:

"The whole system of decisions applicable to this subject rests on the law of nations as its base."

He then turned directly to Vattel:

"Vattel, who, though not very full to this point, is more explicit and more satisfactory on it than any other whose work has fallen into my hands."

Marshall then quoted Section 212 of Vattel:

"The citizens are the members of the civil society; bound to this society by certain duties, and subject to its authority, they equally participate in its advantages. The natives or indigenes are those born in the country of parents who are citizens..."[105]

This citation is significant. Marshall did not reference Vattel casually. He described him as "more explicit and more satisfactory" than other authorities and relied upon him when discussing citizenship and national character.

It is historically noteworthy that Marshall had studied under George Wythe at William & Mary, where Vattel's *Law of Nations* was used as a textbook. Whether as student or jurist, Marshall clearly regarded Vattel as authoritative in matters touching citizenship and allegiance.

One year later, in *The Nereide* (1815),[106] the Supreme Court again

104 *The Venus*, 12 U.S. (8 Cranch) 253 (1814)
105 Emer de Vattel, *The Law of Nations* (1758), bk. I, Ch. 19, § 212.
106 See, e.g., *The Nereide*, 13 U.S. (9 Cranch) 388 (1815).

addressed issues arising under *The Law of Nations*. Chief Justice Marshall stated unequivocally:

"The Court is bound by the law of nations, which is a part of the law of the land."[107]

This statement is direct and categorical.

Marshall did not describe *The Law of Nations* as advisory. He described it as binding, "part of the law of the land." In the absence of contrary congressional enactment, the Court considered itself obligated to apply it.

Taken together, these decisions confirm that, in the early nineteenth century, the Supreme Court recognized *The Law of Nations* as an operative component of American law and relied upon Vattel as an authoritative source when defining concepts such as citizenship and national character.

In 1856, Democrat James Buchanan won the presidential election and was inaugurated on March 4, 1857. Just two days later, on March 6, 1857, the Supreme Court issued its decision in the case of *Scott v. Sandford*[108] (commonly referred to as Dred Scott), holding that persons of African descent could not be citizens of the United States and therefore lacked standing to sue in federal court.

Chief Justice Roger Taney hoped the decision would resolve the escalating national controversy over slavery. Instead, it intensified division and inflamed public opinion nationwide.

The backlash was immediate and fierce. Republican newspaper editor Horace Greeley, founder of the *New York Tribune*, published pamphlets featuring Justice Benjamin Curtis's dissenting opinion[109] to influence the elections of 1858 and 1860. Curtis had forcefully rejected the majority's citizenship analysis.

The Republican Party, running on a platform opposing the

107 Ibid.

108 Scott v. Sandford, 60 U.S. (19 How.) 393 (1857).

109 Benjamin R. Curtis, dissenting opinion in *Scott v. Sandford*, 60 U.S. (19 How.) 393 (1857).

expansion of slavery, elected Abraham Lincoln in 1860. Lincoln was inaugurated on March 4, 1861. One month later, on April 12, 1861, Confederate forces fired upon Fort Sumter, marking the beginning of the Civil War.

The war would last four years and claim more than 750,000 lives, approximately two percent of the nation's population.

Even before the Emancipation Proclamation, Congress was actively debating measures to abolish slavery in federal territories. *The Congressional Globe* records discussion of legislation to end "Slavery in the District" of Columbia[110] — signaling that the federal government was beginning to confront the legal and constitutional implications of slavery and citizenship directly.

In the aftermath of the Civil War, Congress confronted directly the constitutional failures exposed by Dred Scott. The question of citizenship could no longer remain ambiguous.

During debates recorded in the *Congressional Globe*, Representative John Bingham, a principal framer of the future Fourteenth Amendment, addressed the meaning of "natural-born citizen."

Bingham stated:

"The Constitution leaves no room for doubt upon this subject. The words 'natural-born citizen of the United States' occur in it, and the other provision also occurs in it that 'Congress shall have power to pass a uniform system of naturalization.' To naturalize a person is to admit him to citizenship. Who are natural-born citizens but those born within the Republic? Those born within the Republic, whether black or white, are citizens by birth, natural-born citizens. There is no such word as white in your Constitution. Citizenship, therefore, does not depend upon complexion…"

He continued:

110 *Congressional Globe,* debates of the 37th Congress https://digital.library.unt.edu/ark:/67531/metapth2367/m1/237/

"All from other lands, who, by the terms of your laws and a compliance with their provisions, become naturalized, are adopted citizens of the United States; all other persons born within the Republic, of parents owing allegiance to no other sovereignty, are natural-born citizens. Gentlemen can find no exception to this statement touching natural-born citizens except what is said in the Constitution relating to Indians."[111]

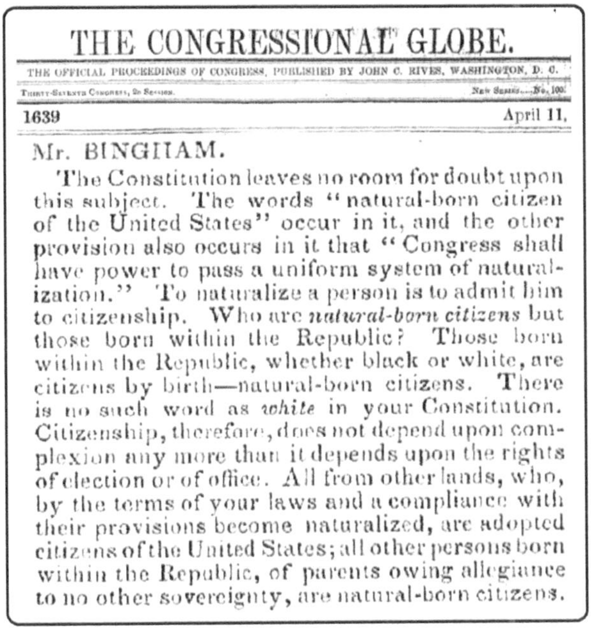

THE CONGRESSIONAL GLOBE.

THE OFFICIAL PROCEEDINGS OF CONGRESS, PUBLISHED BY JOHN C. RIVES, WASHINGTON, D. C.

THIRTY-SEVENTH CONGRESS, 2D SESSION. NEW SERIES....No. 103.

1639 April 11.

Mr. BINGHAM.

The Constitution leaves no room for doubt upon this subject. The words "natural-born citizen of the United States" occur in it, and the other provision also occurs in it that "Congress shall have power to pass a uniform system of naturalization." To naturalize a person is to admit him to citizenship. Who are *natural-born citizens* but those born within the Republic? Those born within the Republic, whether black or white, are citizens by birth—natural-born citizens. There is no such word as *white* in your Constitution. Citizenship, therefore, does not depend upon complexion any more than it depends upon the rights of election or of office. All from other lands, who, by the terms of your laws and a compliance with their provisions become naturalized, are adopted citizens of the United States; all other persons born within the Republic, of parents owing allegiance to no other sovereignty, are natural-born citizens.

This statement is significant for several reasons.

First, Bingham distinguishes clearly between:

- Natural-born citizens
- Naturalized (or "adopted") citizens.

Second, he ties natural-born citizenship to birth within the Republic to parents "owing allegiance to no other sovereignty."[112]

Third, he explicitly references the constitutional language itself, indicating that the Reconstruction Congress was conscious of the

111 John A. Bingham, remarks in *Congressional Globe*, 39th Cong., 1st sess. (1866).

112 Ibid. https://web.archive.org/web/20210222182837/http:/memory.loc.gov/cgi-bin/ampage?collId=llcg&fileName=059/llcg059.db&recNum=680

distinction embedded in Article II.

Bingham's remarks demonstrate that, even during Reconstruction, after the trauma of the Civil War and in the wake of Dred Scott, lawmakers continued to speak of natural-born citizenship in terms that linked birth and allegiance.

Congressional debates during the Civil War era confirm that lawmakers distinguished between two categories of citizenship: those born citizens and those who became citizens through naturalization.

Members of Congress repeatedly referenced the constitutional distinction between "natural-born citizens" and naturalized citizens, reflecting the language of Article II and Article I's grant of power to Congress "to establish a uniform Rule of Naturalization."

This distinction was not treated as incidental. It was understood as foundational to the Constitution's structure of citizenship.

Four months later, on September 22, 1862, President Abraham Lincoln issued the preliminary Emancipation Proclamation, declaring that slavery would be abolished in the rebelling states effective January 1, 1863. The Proclamation applied only to states in rebellion and did not immediately end slavery in Union states.

The constitutional questions of citizenship, allegiance, and civil status, therefore, remained unsettled. Congress would soon confront these questions directly in legislation that reshaped the legal landscape of citizenship in the United States.

On December 8, 1863, President Abraham Lincoln issued the Proclamation of Amnesty and Reconstruction, signaling the beginning of the Reconstruction Era. Congress was now tasked not only with ending slavery but with determining the civil and political status of millions of newly freed individuals.

In January 1864, Senator Lyman Trumbull introduced what would become the Thirteenth Amendment. The amendment passed the Senate on April 8, 1864, the House on January 31, 1865, and was ratified on December 6, 1865, abolishing slavery throughout the United States.

Tragically, days after the passage of the amendment, President Lincoln was assassinated on April 14, 1865, in Washington, D.C., at Ford's Theatre, where he was attending a play. He was shot by Confederate sympathizer John Wilkes Booth and died the next morning, April 15, 1865. The assassination occurred in the closing days of the Civil War, as Lincoln sought to reunify the nation and advance Reconstruction policies, and was motivated by Booth's opposition to Lincoln's leadership and the Union victory.

Vice President Andrew Johnson assumed the presidency amid a deeply divided nation. Despite political turbulence, Congress continued grappling with questions of citizenship, allegiance, and civil integration of millions of future-to-be formerly enslaved people.

During this same period, courts continued to reference *The Law of Nations* as authoritative guidance on citizenship.

In *Meares v. Sinclair et al.* (West Virginia Supreme Court of Appeals, 1865), the court addressed questions involving domicile and citizenship. In discussing the "test of citizenship," the court cited multiple authorities, including Vattel:

"Test of citizenship. 1 Kent, 82, 83, 86. Vattel, 101, §§ 212, 213, 214..."[113]

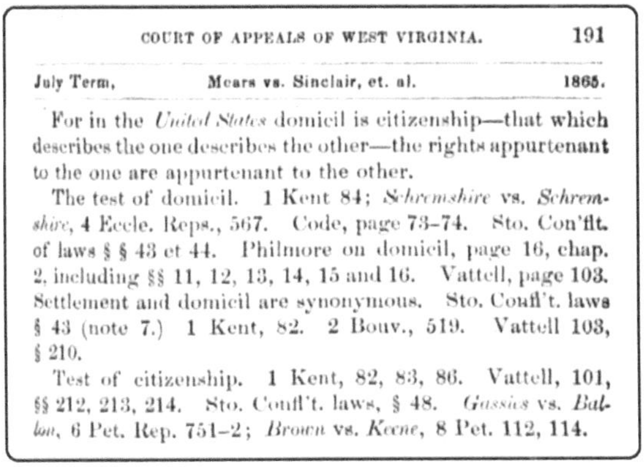
COURT OF APPEALS OF WEST VIRGINIA. 191

July Term, Mears vs. Sinclair, et. al. 1865.

For in the *United States* domicil is citizenship—that which describes the one describes the other—the rights appurtenant to the one are appurtenant to the other.

The test of domicil. 1 Kent 84; *Schremshire* vs. *Schremshire*, 4 Eccle. Reps., 567. Code, page 73–74. Sto. Con'flt. of laws § § 43 et 44. Philmore on domicil, page 16, chap. 2, including §§ 11, 12, 13, 14, 15 and 16. Vattell, page 103. Settlement and domicil are synonymous. Sto. Confl't. laws § 43 (note 7.) 1 Kent, 82. 2 Bouv., 519. Vattell 103, § 210.

Test of citizenship. 1 Kent, 82, 83, 86. Vattell, 101, §§ 212, 213, 214. Sto. Confl't. laws, § 48. *Gassies* vs. *Ballon*, 6 Pet. Rep. 751–2; *Brown* vs. *Keene*, 8 Pet. 112, 114.

113 Reports of Cases Decided in the Supreme Court of Appeals of West Virginia Volume https://books.google.com/books?id=oKwUAAAAYAAJ&dq=%22vattell%22&pg=RA1-PA191#v=onepage&q=%22vattell%22&f=false

The court also referenced Vattel in connection with domicile and settlement, alongside Kent and Story.

This citation is significant for several reasons.

First, it demonstrates that, during Reconstruction, in the very moment Congress was redefining citizenship at the federal level, state courts continued to treat Vattel as an authoritative source on citizenship and domicile.

Second, the court specifically cited Sections 212–214 of Vattel, the same sections defining citizens and natives.

Third, Vattel appears not as a historical curiosity but alongside Kent and Story as foundational American legal commentators.

Even in 1865, therefore, American courts continued to consult Vattel when addressing questions of citizenship and political status.

Although the Thirteenth Amendment abolished slavery, a profound constitutional question remained unresolved: the status of millions of formerly enslaved people who had been denied citizenship under *Dred Scott v. Sandford*.

The Court's 1857 decision had declared that persons of African descent could not be citizens of the United States. With slavery now abolished, Congress faced the urgent task of determining the civil and political status of those who had been excluded from national membership.

Public pressure mounted. The nation demanded clarity.

On December 4, 1865, Congress appointed a Joint Committee on Reconstruction, composed of fifteen members, six from the Senate and nine from the House of Representatives, to examine the condition of the former Confederate states and to recommend measures necessary for reintegration and constitutional reform.

The House members included Thaddeus Stevens (Pennsylvania), John Bingham (Ohio), Justin Morrill (Vermont), Elihu Washburne

(Illinois), Henry Grider (Kentucky), Roscoe Conkling (New York), George Boutwell (Massachusetts), Henry Blow (Missouri), and Andrew Jackson Rogers (New Jersey).[114]

The Senate members included William P. Fessenden (Maine), James W. Grimes (Iowa), Ira Harris (New York), Jacob Howard (Michigan), Reverdy Johnson (Maryland), and George H. Williams (Oregon).[115]

This committee would become instrumental in shaping the Civil Rights Act of 1866 and the Fourteenth Amendment, the two most consequential legislative efforts to redefine citizenship in American history.

The Reconstruction Congress was not operating in a vacuum. It inherited an existing constitutional framework, longstanding debates over allegiance, and a judicial tradition that recognized *The Law of Nations* as part of the law of the land.

The question before Congress was not whether citizenship existed, but how it was to be defined in a post-slavery republic.

The Joint Committee on Reconstruction conducted extensive investigations into conditions in the former Confederate states. The Committee gathered testimony from freedmen, military officers, and former Confederate officials concerning civil rights, political participation, and the treatment of newly emancipated people.

The Committee's findings would help shape the Civil Rights Act of 1866[116], the first major legislative effort to define national citizenship following the abolition of slavery.

Authored by Senator Lyman Trumbull, the Civil Rights Act was introduced in the Senate on January 5, 1866. It passed the Senate on

---

114 https://tile.loc.gov/image-services/iiif/public:gdcmassbookdig:journalofjointco01unit:journalofjointco01unit_0007/full/pct:50.0/0/default.jpg

115 https://tile.loc.gov/image-services/iiif/public:gdcmassbookdig:journalofjointco01unit:journalofjointco01unit_0008/full/pct:50.0/0/default.jpg

116 Civil Rights Act of 1866, Ch. 31, 14 Stat. 27.

February 2, 1866, and was then sent to the House of Representatives for debate.

During House discussions on March 9, 1866, Representative John Bingham, later recognized as a principal framer of the Fourteenth Amendment, addressed Section 1 of the bill regarding citizenship.

Bingham stated:

"I find no fault with the introductory clause, which is simply declaratory of what is written in the Constitution, that every human being born within the jurisdiction of the United States of parents not owing allegiance to any foreign sovereignty is, in the language of your Constitution itself, a natural-born citizen."

The Civil Rights Act of 1866 defined citizens as those "born in the United States and not subject to any foreign power."[117] This language reflects an allegiance-based understanding of citizenship, excluding those owing political loyalty to a foreign sovereign. When the Fourteenth Amendment was later adopted, it constitutionalized citizenship using the phrase "subject to the jurisdiction thereof." Although the wording differs from that of the Civil Rights Act, the debates reveal that Congress was addressing general national citizenship, not the distinct presidential eligibility requirement under Article II.

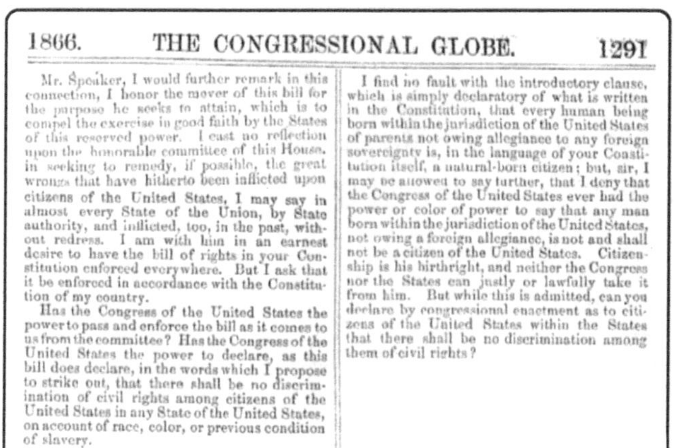

1866. THE CONGRESSIONAL GLOBE. 1291

Mr. Speaker, I would further remark in this connection, I honor the mover of this bill for the purpose he seeks to attain, which is to compel the exercise in good faith by the States of this reserved power. I cast no reflection upon the honorable committee of this House, in seeking to remedy, if possible, the great wrongs that have hitherto been inflicted upon citizens of the United States, I may say in almost every State of the Union, by State authority, and inflicted, too, in the past, without redress. I am with him in an earnest desire to have the bill of rights in your Constitution enforced everywhere. But I ask that it be enforced in accordance with the Constitution of my country.

Has the Congress of the United States the power to pass and enforce the bill as it comes to us from the committee? Has the Congress of the United States the power to declare, as this bill does declare, in the words which I propose to strike out, that there shall be no discrimination of civil rights among citizens of the United States in any State of the United States, on account of race, color, or previous condition of slavery.

I find no fault with the introductory clause, which is simply declaratory of what is written in the Constitution, that every human being born within the jurisdiction of the United States of parents not owing allegiance to any foreign sovereignty is, in the language of your Constitution itself, a natural-born citizen; but, sir, I may be allowed to say further, that I deny that the Congress of the United States ever had the power or color of power to say that any man born within the jurisdiction of the United States, not owing a foreign allegiance, is not and shall not be a citizen of the United States. Citizenship is his birthright, and neither the Congress nor the States can justly or lawfully take it from him. But while this is admitted, can you declare by congressional enactment as to citizens of the United States within the States that there shall be no discrimination among them of civil rights?

117 Ibid.

The Fourteenth Amendment does not use the phrase "natural-born citizen," nor does it amend Article II. It establishes who is a citizen of the United States, but it does not redefine the separate constitutional qualification for the presidency.

Thus, while Reconstruction reshaped national citizenship, it left untouched the specific requirement that the President be a "natural-born Citizen."

This statement is significant for several reasons.

First, Bingham characterizes the language as "declaratory of what is written in the Constitution," not as an invention.

Second, he links birth within the jurisdiction to parents "not owing allegiance to any foreign sovereignty."

Third, he explicitly equates this status with the constitutional phrase "natural-born citizen."

In the Reconstruction Congress, nearly 80 years after the Constitutional Convention, lawmakers were still discussing natural-born citizenship in terms that combined birth within the jurisdiction with allegiance.

Section 1 of the Civil Rights Act of 1866 provided:

"All persons born in the United States and not subject to any foreign power, excluding Indians not taxed, are hereby declared to be citizens of the United States."[118]

THIRTY-NINTH CONGRESS. Sess. I. Ch. 31. 1866. 27

CHAP. XXXI. — *An Act to protect all Persons in the United States in their Civil Rights, and furnish the Means of their Vindication.* April 9, 1866.

Be it enacted by the Senate and House of Representatives of the United States of America in Congress assembled, That all persons born in the United States and not subject to any foreign power, excluding Indians not taxed, are hereby declared to be citizens of the United States; Who are citizens of the United States,

The language "not subject to any foreign power" is significant. It reflects the longstanding understanding that citizenship required not merely birth within territorial limits, but birth free of foreign

118 Civil Rights Act of 1866, Ch. 31, § 1, 14 Stat. 27 (Apr. 9, 1866).

allegiance. Congress in 1866 was legislating against the backdrop of Dred Scott and in light of existing constitutional terminology, including Article II's "natural-born citizen" requirement. The Act, therefore, did not create a new theory of citizenship; rather, it articulated in statutory form what Congress understood to be the existing rule governing birth and allegiance within the United States.

For the first time in federal statutory law, Congress formally defined national citizenship. The requirement that a person be "born in the United States and not subject to any foreign power" reflects an allegiance-based understanding of political membership.

The phrase "not subject to any foreign power" echoes longstanding discussions of sovereignty and allegiance found in eighteenth-century law-of-nations treatises, including Vattel's *Law of Nations*. While the Act does not cite Vattel directly, the definition's structure parallels the earlier framework that ties citizenship to birth and exclusive political allegiance.

This Act did not amend Article II. It did not define "natural-born Citizen." It defined who is a citizen of the United States for purposes of civil rights protection. Nevertheless, its allegiance requirement is critical in understanding how Congress, in 1866, understood political membership and sovereignty.

On February 28, 1866, just days after the Civil Rights Act passed in the Senate, Representative John Bingham of Ohio introduced an original draft of what would later become the Fourteenth Amendment. Many members of Congress questioned whether the Civil Rights Act alone was constitutionally secure. Bingham sought to embed its core protections within the Constitution itself.

Although his initial proposal did not advance, his speech during the debate is significant. In defending the legitimacy of constitutional authority and Reconstruction measures, Bingham invoked the same philosophical foundation articulated by the Founders:

"...the right of the people to self-preservation justifies it; it rests upon the transcendent right of nature and nature's God. That right is still in the people... It is the inherent right of the people. It cannot be taken from them."[119]

Bingham's language demonstrates that even during Reconstruction, members of Congress continued to ground constitutional authority in the principles of natural law and the sovereignty of the people.

Bingham's rejected original draft used language similar to Article IV of the Constitution, language that was removed during subsequent revisions. His later draft of the Fourteenth Amendment would instead establish what became the Privileges or Immunities Clause and the Equal Protection Clause.

The original proposed text of Section 1 read:

Section 1 – Original Draft:

"The Congress shall have power to make all laws which shall be necessary and proper to secure to the citizens of each State all privileges and immunities of citizens in the several States, and to all persons in the several States equal protection in the rights of life, liberty, and property."

Because the Civil Rights Act of 1866 and the Fourteenth Amendment were developed by many of the same members of Congress; the Amendment's citizenship clause closely mirrors the language of the Act. Likewise, the Privileges or Immunities and Equal Protection clauses reflect the Act's non-discrimination provisions. While some considered the Amendment redundant, its ratification ensured that the principles of the 1866 Act would be constitutionally secured against repeal.

After difficulty advancing the initial proposal, the bill was returned to the Reconstruction Committee for revision. Senator Lyman Trumbull, the author of the Civil Rights Act, worked with

---

119 John A. Bingham, speech in Congressional Globe, 39th Cong., 1st sess. (1866).

Senator Jacob Howard in refining the language. It was during this revision process that the citizenship clause was incorporated into the Amendment in its now-familiar form.

The revised text of Section 1 reads:

"All persons born or naturalized in the United States, and subject to the jurisdiction thereof, are citizens of the United States and of the State wherein they reside. No State shall make or enforce any law which shall abridge the privileges or immunities of citizens of the United States; nor shall any State deprive any person of life, liberty, or property, without due process of law; nor deny to any person within its jurisdiction the equal protection of the laws."[120]

Some have argued that the Fourteenth Amendment created a new or updated definition of citizenship based solely on territorial birth. However, during debate, Senator Jacob Howard described the citizenship clause as:

"Simply declaratory of what I regard as the law of the land already, that every person born within the limits of the United States, and subject to their jurisdiction, is by virtue of natural law and national law a citizen of the United States."[121]

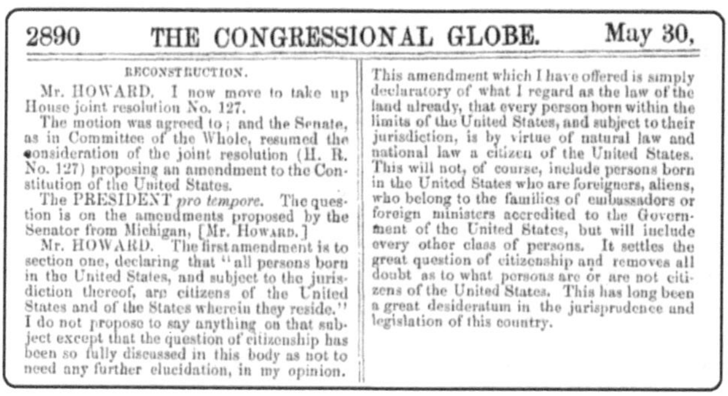
2890 THE CONGRESSIONAL GLOBE. May 30,

RECONSTRUCTION.

Mr. HOWARD. I now move to take up House joint resolution No. 127.

The motion was agreed to; and the Senate, as in Committee of the Whole, resumed the consideration of the joint resolution (H. R. No. 127) proposing an amendment to the Constitution of the United States.

The PRESIDENT *pro tempore*. The question is on the amendments proposed by the Senator from Michigan, [Mr. Howard.]

Mr. HOWARD. The first amendment is to section one, declaring that "all persons born in the United States, and subject to the jurisdiction thereof, are citizens of the United States and of the States wherein they reside." I do not propose to say anything on that subject except that the question of citizenship has been so fully discussed in this body as not to need any further elucidation, in my opinion. This amendment which I have offered is simply declaratory of what I regard as the law of the land already, that every person born within the limits of the United States, and subject to their jurisdiction, is by virtue of natural law and national law a citizen of the United States. This will not, of course, include persons born in the United States who are foreigners, aliens, who belong to the families of embassadors or foreign ministers accredited to the Government of the United States, but will include every other class of persons. It settles the great question of citizenship and removes all doubt as to what persons are or are not citizens of the United States. This has long been a great desideratum in the jurisprudence and legislation of this country.

Howard's remarks are significant. He did not characterize the clause as creating a new theory of citizenship. Rather, he described it as affirming what he believed to be existing law, grounded in both natural law and national law.

120 U.S. Const. amend. XIV, § 1.

121 Jacob Howard, remarks introducing the Fourteenth Amendment, *Congressional Globe,* 39th Cong., 1st sess. (1866).

This framing becomes especially important when examining how Reconstruction-era lawmakers understood citizenship, allegiance, and jurisdiction within the constitutional structure.

Also, during the debates over the Fourteenth Amendment, senators directly questioned the meaning of the phrase "subject to the jurisdiction thereof." The phrase was not left unexplained.

Senator Lyman Trumbull, author of the Civil Rights Act of 1866 and a central figure in incorporating the citizenship clause into the Amendment, addressed the issue plainly on the Senate floor. He stated:

"The provision is that 'all persons born in the United States, and subject to the jurisdiction thereof, are citizens.' That means 'subject to the complete jurisdiction thereof.' Now, does the Senator from Wisconsin pretend to say that the Navajo Indians are subject to the complete jurisdiction of the United States? ... What do we mean by 'subject to the jurisdiction of the United States'? Not owing allegiance to anybody else. That is what it means."[122]

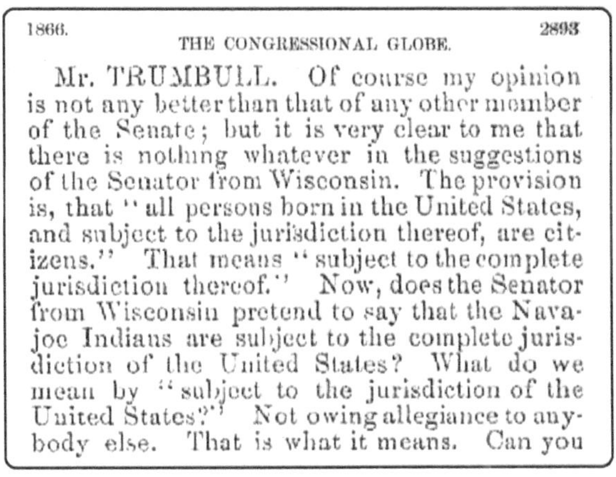

1866. THE CONGRESSIONAL GLOBE. 2893

Mr. TRUMBULL. Of course my opinion is not any better than that of any other member of the Senate; but it is very clear to me that there is nothing whatever in the suggestions of the Senator from Wisconsin. The provision is, that "all persons born in the United States, and subject to the jurisdiction thereof, are citizens." That means "subject to the complete jurisdiction thereof." Now, does the Senator from Wisconsin pretend to say that the Navajoe Indians are subject to the complete jurisdiction of the United States? What do we mean by "subject to the jurisdiction of the United States?" Not owing allegiance to anybody else. That is what it means. Can you

Trumbull's clarification is significant. He equated "subject to the jurisdiction thereof" with "complete jurisdiction," and he defined that complete jurisdiction as not owing allegiance to any foreign power.

122 Lyman Trumbull, remarks on citizenship clause, *Congressional Globe,* 39th Cong., 1st sess., 2893 (1866).

This language closely parallels the wording of the Civil Rights Act of 1866, which defined citizens as those "born in the United States and not subject to any foreign power."

The debates, therefore, indicate that the Reconstruction Congress did not treat the Fourteenth Amendment's citizenship clause as introducing a novel theory of citizenship. Rather, they described it as articulating, in constitutional form, the same allegiance-based principle that had already been expressed in statutory language.

Whether one agrees with that interpretation or not, the record shows that the framers of the Amendment themselves understood "subject to the jurisdiction thereof" as involving the question of allegiance.

After undergoing debate and revision, the Fourteenth Amendment passed the Senate on June 8, 1866. The House approved the amendment shortly thereafter on June 13, 1866. It was then submitted to the states for ratification. On July 27, 1868, Secretary of State William H. Seward officially proclaimed the Fourteenth Amendment to be adopted as part of the Constitution.

Two years later, Congress enacted the Enforcement Act of 1870.[123] Section 18 of that Act expressly reenacted the Civil Rights Act of 1866. The statute provided that the 1866 Act was "hereby re-enacted," reinforcing its operative provisions.

May 31, 1870. CHAP. CXIV.—*An Act to enforce the Right of Citizens of the United States to vote in the several States of this Union, and for other Purposes.*

144 FORTY-FIRST CONGRESS. Sess. II. Ch. 114. 1870.

Civil rights bill re-enacted. 1866, ch. 31. Vol. xiv. p. 27.

Sec. 18. *And be it further enacted*, That the act to protect all persons in the United States in their civil rights, and furnish the means of their vindication, passed April nine, eighteen hundred and sixty-six, is hereby re-enacted; and sections sixteen and seventeen hereof shall be enforced according to the provisions of said act.

The reenactment is notable. By restating the Civil Rights Act after the ratification of the Fourteenth Amendment, Congress signaled that the statutory definition of citizenship remained operative and consistent with the constitutional amendment. The

123 Enforcement Act of 1870, Ch. 114, 16 Stat. 140. https://www.senate.gov/artandhistory/history/resources/pdf/EnforcementAct_1870.pdf

citizenship language originally enacted in 1866, including its allegiance requirement, was not discarded.

From this sequence, it is argued that the Fourteenth Amendment did not fundamentally alter the existing understanding of citizenship articulated in the Civil Rights Act. Instead, the Amendment constitutionalized protections while Congress reaffirmed the statutory framework through reenactment.

For those who ground citizenship in principles of natural law, the argument follows that such foundational concepts are not subject to ordinary legislative revision, but instead reflect enduring principles understood to preexist statutory enactment.

The reenactment of the Civil Rights Act in 1870 invites reconsideration of the earlier Reconstruction debates. If Congress had understood the Fourteenth Amendment to alter the allegiance-based language of the 1866 Act fundamentally, reenactment would have required modification. Instead, Congress reaffirmed the statutory text. This sequence suggests continuity rather than rupture in the understanding of citizenship during Reconstruction.

Three years after the ratification of the Fourteenth Amendment, the Supreme Court addressed its meaning in The *Slaughter-House Cases* (1873).[124]

These consolidated cases arose from a challenge by New Orleans butchers who claimed that a state-created monopoly violated the Fourteenth Amendment's Privileges or Immunities Clause.

While the core issue involved economic regulation, the Court necessarily examined the Fourteenth Amendment's citizenship clause.

Justice Samuel Miller, writing for the majority, stated:

"It overturns the Dred Scott decision by making all persons born within the United States and subject to its jurisdiction citizens

124 *The Slaughter-House Cases*, 83 U.S. (16 Wall.) 36 (1873).

of the United States. That its main purpose was to establish the citizenship of the negro can admit of no doubt. The phrase, 'subject to its jurisdiction,' was intended to exclude from its operation children of ministers, consuls, and citizens or subjects of foreign States born within the United States."[125]

This language mirrors the explanation given by Senator Trumbull during the 1866 debates that "subject to the jurisdiction" meant complete jurisdiction and not owing allegiance to any foreign power.

Thus, within five years of ratification, the Supreme Court itself interpreted the jurisdiction clause as requiring full political allegiance, not mere territorial presence.

Just two years after *The Slaughter-House Cases*, the Supreme Court again addressed the question of citizenship in *Minor v. Happersett.*[126] The case concerned whether the Fourteenth Amendment granted women the right to vote. Although the Court ultimately held that citizenship did not automatically confer suffrage, it first examined the meaning of citizenship itself.

Chief Justice Morrison Waite acknowledged that the Constitution does not expressly define who qualifies as a "natural-born citizen." He wrote:

"The Constitution does not, in words, say who shall be natural-born citizens. Resort must be had elsewhere to ascertain that."[127]

The Court then turned to the common-law understanding familiar to the Framers:

"At common law, with the nomenclature of which the framers of the Constitution were familiar, it was never doubted that all children born in a country of parents who were its citizens became themselves, upon their birth, citizens also. These were natives, or natural-born citizens, as distinguished from aliens or foreigners."[128]

---

125 Ibid.

126 *Minor v. Happersett,* 88 U.S. (21 Wall.) 162 (1875).

127 Ibid.

128 Ibid.

Several points are significant.

First, the Court distinguished between citizens by birth and citizens by naturalization. Justice Waite stated plainly:

"Additions might always be made to the citizenship of the United States in two ways: first, by birth, and second, by naturalization."

Second, in describing those who were "never doubted" to be natural-born citizens, the Court referenced children born in a country to parents who were its citizens. These individuals were described as "natives, or natural-born citizens," as distinguished from "aliens or foreigners."

The Court did not need to resolve whether other classes of persons born within the United States might also qualify as natural-born citizens, because the issue before it concerned voting rights, not presidential eligibility. Nevertheless, the Court's articulation of the undisputed core category of natural-born citizens is historically important.

By 1875, nearly a century after the Constitution was drafted, the Supreme Court acknowledged that, according to the Framers' understanding, children born in the country to citizen parents were unquestionably natural-born citizens.

This description is consistent with earlier references to allegiance, political jurisdiction, and the distinction between natural-born and naturalized citizens found throughout the Reconstruction debates and earlier constitutional commentary.

Furthermore, just four years after the 1870 Enforcement Act re-enacted the 1866 Civil Rights Act, and one year after both *The Slaughter-House Cases* (1873) *and Minor v. Happersett* (1875) addressed citizenship, Congress published the Revised Statutes of the United States (1873–74).

These statutes consolidated the general and permanent laws of the United States then in force. In doing so, Congress once again codified the definition of citizenship in the 1866 Civil Rights Act.

Title XXV, Citizenship, Section 1992 states:

"All persons born in the United States and not subject to any foreign power, excluding Indians not taxed, are hereby declared to be citizens of the United States."[129]

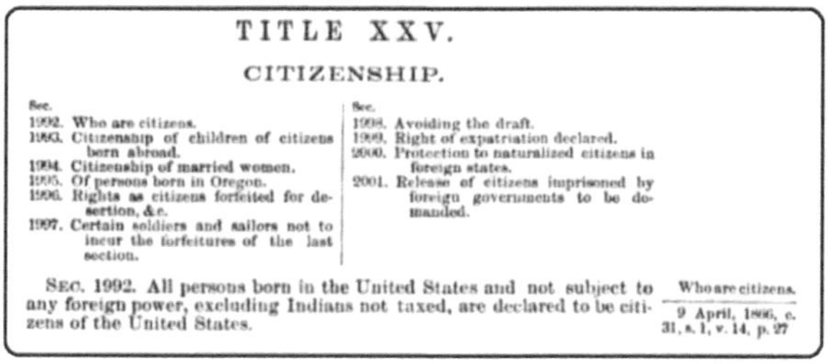

TITLE XXV.

CITIZENSHIP.

Sec.
1992. Who are citizens.
1993. Citizenship of children of citizens born abroad.
1994. Citizenship of married women.
1995. Of persons born in Oregon.
1996. Rights as citizens forfeited for desertion, &c.
1997. Certain soldiers and sailors not to incur the forfeitures of the last section.

Sec.
1998. Avoiding the draft.
1999. Right of expatriation declared.
2000. Protection to naturalized citizens in foreign states.
2001. Release of citizens imprisoned by foreign governments to be demanded.

SEC. 1992. All persons born in the United States and not subject to any foreign power, excluding Indians not taxed, are declared to be citizens of the United States.

Who are citizens.

9 April, 1866, c. 31, s. 1, v. 14, p. 27

This language is identical to Section 1 of the Civil Rights Act of 1866.

Notably, the margin citation explicitly references:

"9 April 1866."

— the original enactment date of the Civil Rights Act.

This is now the third federal reaffirmation of the same citizenship definition:

Civil Rights Act of 1866

Enforcement Act of 1870 (re-enactment)

Revised Statutes of 1873–74, §1992

The continuity is unmistakable. Congress did not alter the "not subject to any foreign power" language after the ratification of the Fourteenth Amendment. Instead, it preserved and re-codified it.

This statutory repetition demonstrates that, in the years immediately following the Fourteenth Amendment's adoption, Congress continued to understand citizenship as requiring birth in

129 Revised Statutes of the United States, Title XXV, § 1992 (1873–1874), codifying the citizenship provision of the Civil Rights Act of 1866, Ch. 31, § 1, 14 Stat. 27 (1866).

the United States and freedom from foreign allegiance.

We now arrive at the election of 1880. James Garfield defeated Winfield Scott Hancock, and Garfield's choice for vice president was Chester Alan Arthur. Almost immediately, controversy surrounded Arthur's eligibility.

Garfield was inaugurated on March 4, 1881. After being shot in July and dying from complications on September 19, 1881, Vice President Chester Arthur assumed the presidency.

However, serious allegations regarding Arthur's citizenship circulated during the 1880 campaign and continued after Garfield's death.

The Birthplace Dispute

Multiple reports alleged that Arthur had been born in Dunham Flats, Lower Canada (now Quebec), rather than in Vermont as officially claimed. An 1884 investigation by New York attorney Arthur P. Hinman, titled *"How a British Subject Became President of the United States,"* is one of the most detailed sources advancing this claim.

Hinman's report asserts that:

Arthur was unable to name his birthplace at first when the vice presidential nomination brought public scrutiny.

Party leaders pressured him to provide a birthplace before issuing his letter of acceptance.

Arthur traveled to Montreal to search for records that might confirm whether he had been born in Canada.

Failing to find records establishing a Canadian birth, he allegedly chose a location in Vermont connected to a deceased brother to strengthen the appearance that he was "native born."

Hinman's report cites multiple witnesses who recalled the Arthur family moving frequently across the Vermont–Canada border and who claimed Chester (or an older son) was born in Canada. Other later sources likewise noted that he was "probably born in Canada," though definitive proof is complicated by missing or destroyed records in the relevant towns.

Regardless, the controversy was significant enough to become the subject of a published political and legal investigation during Arthur's presidency.

The Father's Citizenship and Naturalization:

Even setting aside the birthplace issue, another citizenship question remains.

Chester Arthur's father, William Arthur, was born in Ireland and later lived in Canada before relocating to the United States. Critically, documentary evidence shows that William Arthur did not become a United States citizen until 1843.[130]

The Washington County, New York, naturalization record (shown below) certifies that William Arthur was admitted and became a "Citizen of the United States" on August 3, 1843.

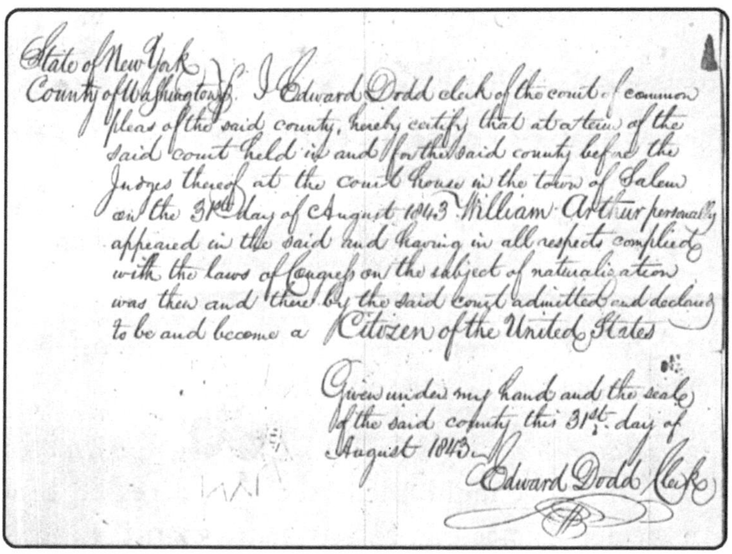

State of New York
County of Washington ss. I Edward Dodd clerk of the court of common pleas of the said county, hereby certify that at a term of the said court held in and for the said county before the Judges thereof at the court house in the town of Salem on the 31st day of August 1843 William Arthur personally appeared in the said court and having in all respects complied with the laws of Congress on the subject of naturalization was then and there by the said court admitted and declared to be and become a Citizen of the United States

Given under my hand and the seal of the said county this 31st day of August 1843

Edward Dodd Clerk

130 Washington County, New York Naturalization Record, William Arthur, admitted August 3, 1843.

That matters because Chester Arthur's birth year is generally placed in the late 1820s or 1830s. Either way, Chester was born more than a decade before his father was naturalized, meaning his father was not a U.S. citizen at the time of Chester's birth.

The Constitutional Question:

If natural-born citizenship is understood as requiring allegiance from birth and descent from citizen parents, then William Arthur's non-citizenship at the time of Chester's birth becomes central.

Under that interpretation:

If Chester Arthur was born in Canada, he was born a British subject.

If he was born in Vermont, he was still born to a father who was not yet a U.S. citizen, as shown by the 1843 naturalization record.

Either way, the eligibility controversy takes on more force when the father's citizenship status is added to the factual timeline.

No court adjudicated Arthur's eligibility at the time. He served from 1881 to 1885. But the episode shows that disputes over presidential eligibility are not modern inventions; they existed in the nineteenth century and were serious enough to trigger formal investigations, public testimony, and searches of documentary records.

Moving forward in the historical record, I came across the 1889 Annotated Statutes of Wisconsin, enacted more than twenty years after the ratification of the Fourteenth Amendment.

On page 15, under the heading "Citizenship and Naturalization," the statute addresses the question "Who are Citizens." The text adopts the same language found in Section 1992 of the Revised Statutes of 1873–74[131] and expressly traces its source to the Civil Rights Act of 1866.

The statute provides:

131 Revised Statutes of the United States (1873–1874), Title XXV, §1992.

"All persons born in the United States and not subject to any foreign power, excluding Indians not taxed, are declared to be citizens of the United States."[132]

ANNOTATED STATUTES

OF

WISCONSIN,

CONTAINING THE

GENERAL LAWS IN FORCE OCTOBER 1, 1889,

CITIZENSHIP AND NATURALIZATION. 15

CITIZENSHIP AND NATURALIZATION.

REVISED STATUTES OF THE UNITED STATES OF 1878.

Who are citizens. SECTION 1992. All persons born in the United States and not subject to any foreign power, excluding Indians not taxed, are declared to be citizens of the United States.

The significance of this enactment is substantial. Even decades after the adoption of the Fourteenth Amendment, legal authorities continued to rely upon and restate the Civil Rights Act definition of citizenship, including its allegiance requirement, without modification.

This continuity demonstrates that the understanding reflected in the Civil Rights Act remained operative in legal and statutory interpretation well into the late nineteenth century, reinforcing the view that the Fourteenth Amendment did not alter the existing framework concerning birth, allegiance, and citizenship.

The controversy surrounding President Chester Arthur is relevant because it intersects with one of the most frequently cited Supreme Court cases in modern citizenship debates: *United States v. Wong Kim Ark.*[133]

That decision is often invoked to support a broad interpretation

---

132 Annotated Statutes of Wisconsin (1889), Citizenship and Naturalization, adopting Rev. Stat. §1992 language.

133 *United States v. Wong Kim Ark,* 169 U.S. 649 (1898).

of birthright citizenship under the Fourteenth Amendment. However, a careful reading of the case reveals two important points.

First, Wong Kim Ark did not interpret Article II of the Constitution or define the term "natural-born citizen." The term "natural-born citizen" was not even mentioned once in the entire text. The case addressed only whether a person born in the United States to foreign parents was a citizen under the Fourteenth Amendment's Citizenship Clause. Presidential eligibility was not before the Court.

Second and the far more revealing point is the dissent authored by Chief Justice Melville Fuller and joined by Justice John Marshall Harlan.[134]

The dissent rejects the majority's heavy reliance on English common-law jus soli and instead grounds citizenship in principles of allegiance consistent with the law of nations. The dissent argues that mere birth within territorial limits is insufficient where political allegiance is absent. It emphasizes that children born to parents who owe allegiance to a foreign sovereign inherit that allegiance at birth.

Chief Justice Fuller wrote that the majority had adopted a theory of citizenship that diverged from the understanding rooted in American sovereignty and the law of nations. The dissent leaned heavily on Vattel's framework, that citizenship involves political membership tied to allegiance, not merely geography.

This distinction is critical.

The majority opinion interpreted the Fourteenth Amendment's phrase "subject to the jurisdiction thereof" broadly. The dissent, however, interpreted that phrase to require complete political allegiance, not merely territorial subjection.

Thus, even within Wong Kim Ark, the Court itself was divided on whether birth alone was sufficient to establish citizenship when parental allegiance lay elsewhere.

134 *United States v. Wong Kim Ark*, 169 U.S. 649, 705–32 (1898) (Fuller, C.J., dissenting).

Moreover, Wong Kim Ark does not mention the term "natural-born citizen." It does not analyze Article II. It does not purport to define presidential eligibility. It addresses Fourteenth Amendment citizenship only.

The dissent, therefore, remains highly relevant to any discussion of allegiance, sovereignty, and the distinction between birthright citizenship and natural-born citizenship.

Competing Theories in Wong Kim Ark:

The division in Wong Kim Ark can be distilled into two competing constitutional frameworks:

Majority Framework (Justice Gray):

Citizenship under the Fourteenth Amendment follows the English common-law rule of jus soli. Birth within U.S. territorial limits, coupled with being "subject to the jurisdiction thereof," is sufficient to establish citizenship, regardless of parental allegiance (with narrow exceptions such as diplomats and enemy occupiers). However, altering the original meaning of a constitutional amendment through judicial interpretation raises serious constitutional concerns. The role of the courts is to interpret the law according to the intent and understanding of its authors, not to rewrite it. In my view, this is precisely what Justice Gray did. What is even more questionable, Justice Gray was appointed by the ineligible President, Chester Arthur, which should render the decision null and void. You really can't make this stuff up.

Dissenting Framework (Chief Justice Fuller and Justice Harlan):

Citizenship is grounded in political allegiance. The phrase "subject to the jurisdiction thereof" requires complete and undivided allegiance. Children inherit their parents' political conditions at birth. Mere territorial birth is insufficient where parental allegiance lies with a foreign sovereign.

This fundamental disagreement reflects two different conceptions of American citizenship: one territorial, the other allegiance-based.

Even before the Court decided *United States v. Wong Kim Ark*, it had already clarified the meaning of citizenship under the Fourteenth Amendment in ways that emphasized allegiance and political jurisdiction. In *Elk v. Wilkins* (1884),[135] the Supreme Court considered whether John Elk, a Native American who had left his tribe and sought to register to vote in Nebraska, was a citizen of the United States. Elk was denied registration because he had been born owing allegiance to his tribal nation and therefore was not fully subject to the political jurisdiction of the United States at birth.

In its opinion, the Court reiterated the central purpose of the Fourteenth Amendment:

"The main object of the opening sentence of the fourteenth amendment was to settle the question as to the citizenship of free negroes... and to put it beyond doubt that all persons, white or black, and whether formerly slaves or not, born or naturalized in the United States, and owing no allegiance to any alien power, should be citizens of the United States." — *Elk v. Wilkins*, 112 U.S. 94 (1884)

The Court further emphasized:

"This section contemplates two sources of citizenship, and two sources only: birth and naturalization."

And most significantly:

"The evident meaning of these last words is, not merely subject in some respect or degree to the jurisdiction of the United States, but completely subject to their political jurisdiction, and owing them direct and immediate allegiance."

The Court also explicitly referenced Article II, Section 1 of the Constitution, recognizing the distinction between citizenship by birth and citizenship by naturalization:

"The distinction between citizenship by birth and citizenship

135 *Elk v. Wilkins*, 112 U.S. 94 (1884).

by naturalization is clearly marked in the provisions of the Constitution..."

This language reinforces several points already established:

• The Fourteenth Amendment did not erase the distinction between natural-born citizens and naturalized citizens.

• Citizenship under the Amendment requires complete political allegiance.

• Mere territorial presence was insufficient where allegiance lay elsewhere.

In *Elk v. Wilkins*, the Court confirmed that the phrase "subject to the jurisdiction thereof" meant full political allegiance, consistent with earlier statements in *Slaughterhouse*, *Minor v. Happersett*, and the Reconstruction debates of 1866. This language mirrors the explanation given by Senator Trumbull during the 1866 debates that "subject to the jurisdiction" meant complete jurisdiction and not owing allegiance to any foreign power.

Later scholars continued to recognize and openly acknowledge the foundational role that Vattel and *The Law of Nations* played in shaping American constitutional thought, confirming that this influence was understood not only by the Founding generation but by those studying the period decades later.

Taken from the December 1917 meeting of the Colonial Society of Massachusetts, scholars reflecting on the founding period discussed the influence of Vattel's *Law of Nations* on the American Revolution and the framing of the Constitution. Referring to the copies of Vattel sent to Benjamin Franklin in 1775, the Society observed that these works played a meaningful role in shaping American legal and political thought, stating:

"That copy of Vattel, in conjunction with the one in Philadelphia, has a special interest for the student of International Law. For those three books, which arrived here in the early stages of the struggle between the colonies and the motherland, not merely influenced the men who sat in the Continental Congresses in shaping our policy towards Great Britain, but also undoubtedly influenced the framers of the Federal Constitution in the writing of parts of that state document. By the Constitution of the United States, *The Law of Nations* is expressly recognized as being a part of the Law of the land..."[136]

The statement continues by noting that Vattel's treatise was regarded in European foreign offices as a leading authority on international law and that Charles Dumas, who transmitted the copies, helped introduce American statesmen to its principles. The Society further observed that the treatise influenced American policy under Washington and Jefferson and contributed to the development of American understandings of neutrality and relations among nations.

This retrospective assessment, written more than a century after the founding, reflects a scholarly consensus that Vattel's work formed part of the intellectual environment in which the Constitution was framed and early American policy developed.

Beginning in the twentieth century, the Supreme Court continued to reaffirm a principle recognized since the founding: the law of nations forms part of the law of the land of the United States.

In *Banco Nacional de Cuba v. Sabbatino*,[137] Chief Justice Harlan traced this doctrine directly back to the earliest years of the Republic, demonstrating that American courts have long understood the United States to operate within a framework informed by international law principles.

Justice Harlan cited Chief Justice John Jay's statement in *Chisholm v. Georgia*[138]:

"Prior ... to that period [the date of the Constitution], the

136 Transactions of the Colonial Society of Massachusetts, Vol. 19, December Meeting 1917-1919 (Boston: Colonial Society of Massachusetts, 1919), 266.

137 *Banco Nacional de Cuba v. Sabbatino*, 376 U.S. 398 (1964).

138 *Chisholm v. Georgia*, 2 U.S. (2 Dall.) 419 (1793).

United States had, by taking a place among the nations of the earth, become amenable to the law of nations."

He also quoted Justice James Wilson in *Ware v. Hylton*[139]:

"When the United States declared its independence, they were bound to receive the law of nations in its modern state of purity and refinement."

Chief Justice Harlan further pointed to Chief Justice Marshall's declaration in *The Nereide*[140] that:

"The Court is bound by the law of nations, which is a part of the law of the land."

The Court additionally reaffirmed the longstanding interpretive rule that Acts of Congress should never be construed to violate the law of nations if any other construction is reasonably available, citing *MacLeod v. United States* (1913).[141]

These authorities show that the Supreme Court has consistently recognized the law of nations not as abstract philosophy, but as a governing legal principle that informs constitutional interpretation and the legal obligations of the United States within the community of nations.

This continuity, stretching from the founding generation through modern jurisprudence, underscores that the legal framework within which questions of allegiance, sovereignty, and citizenship are understood has always been shaped by principles grounded in the law of nations.

By nature, or according to principles of natural law as understood by the Founding generation, Barack Obama's birth raises questions of divided allegiance that have been the subject of considerable public and scholarly debate. It is well documented that Obama's father was a British subject at the time of Obama's birth. Under the

---

139 *Ware v. Hylton*, 3 U.S. (3 Dall.) 199 (1796).
140 *The Nereide*, 13 U.S. (9 Cranch) 388 (1815).
141 *MacLeod v. United States*, 229 U.S. 416 (1913).

British Nationality Act of 1948,[142] a child born to a father who was a citizen of the United Kingdom and Colonies inherited British nationality by descent.

The British Nationality Act of 1948 provides:

Part II — Citizenship by birth or descent:

5. (1) Subject to the provisions of this section, a person born after the commencement of this Act shall be a citizen of the United Kingdom and Colonies by descent if his father is a citizen of the United Kingdom and Colonies at the time of the birth.

From a historical perspective, this fact is significant because it illustrates that Obama was born with a potential claim of legal allegiance to a foreign sovereignty through his father. Early American sources, including discussions of the law of nations, the Civil Rights Act of 1866, and debates over allegiance, frequently treated freedom from foreign political allegiance as an important consideration in discussions of political membership.

Within a natural law framework, and consistent with historical understandings emphasizing undivided allegiance at birth, circumstances involving foreign nationality at birth have been viewed by some scholars as raising questions about whether such an individual could properly be regarded as a natural-born citizen.[143] At the same time, it is important to note that modern judicial interpretations have often taken a different approach, focusing primarily on the place of birth under constitutional doctrine. The tension between these interpretive traditions forms part of the broader debate examined throughout this work.[144]

Per the historical understanding reflected in the writings of the Founders, the debates of the Reconstruction Congress, and the

142 British Nationality Act 1948, 11 & 12 Geo. 6 c. 56 (U.K.), § 5(1).

143 See generally Jill A. Pryor, "The Natural-born Citizen Clause and Presidential Eligibility: An Approach for Resolving Two Hundred Years of Uncertainty," Yale Law Journal 97 (1988): 881–899.

144 See, e.g., Gabriel J. Chin, "Why Senator John McCain Cannot Be President: Eleven Months and a Hundred Yards Short of Citizenship," Michigan Law Review First Impressions 107 (2008): 1–13.

principles of natural law repeatedly invoked throughout this study, the determining factor for being a "natural-born citizen," as required by Article II of the Constitution, is not merely the place of birth, but the condition of birth.[145]

The question is not simply whether one was born within the territorial limits of the United States, but whether one was born with an undivided political allegiance—that is, whether one was born in the country to parents who were themselves citizens and owed no allegiance to any foreign sovereignty. Under this framework, citizenship by nature flows from the political community through the parents, consistent with the longstanding understanding that political membership is transmitted through allegiance.

Accordingly, after examining the historical record, including the Founding-era sources, early statutes, Reconstruction debates, and subsequent legal developments, the central inquiry regarding presidential eligibility is not merely birthplace, but whether an individual meets the constitutional standard for natural-born citizenship.

Viewed through this lens, questions that have arisen concerning the eligibility of figures such as Chester A. Arthur, Barack Obama, Marco Rubio, Kamala Harris, Nikki Haley, Ted Cruz, George Romney, and others turn not on geography alone, but on the constitutional meaning of natural-born citizenship as understood in light of allegiance, historical practice, and the sources examined throughout this work.

While researching the constitutional meaning of the term "natural-born citizen," I encountered a series of congressional resolutions and proposed amendments spanning several decades. These measures sought either to clarify the meaning of presidential eligibility or to propose changes that would allow individuals who are not natural-born citizens to serve as President.

At first glance, the existence of these proposals raises an

145 See, e.g., James H. Kettner, The Development of American Citizenship, 1608–1870 (Chapel Hill: University of North Carolina Press, 1978).

important constitutional question: how can Congress attempt to alter presidential eligibility without invoking the amendment process required by Article V[146]?

The answer is that Congress cannot change the Constitution by statute. Each of the measures listed below represents either a proposal to amend the Constitution, which would still require ratification by three-fourths of the states, or a nonbinding expression of congressional opinion. Their very existence underscores a crucial point: members of Congress have repeatedly recognized that any alteration to the natural-born-citizen requirement would require a formal constitutional amendment.

Indeed, the recurring introduction of such proposals demonstrates that lawmakers understood Article II to establish a fixed constitutional qualification, one that cannot be modified except through the formal amendment process prescribed by the Constitution.

The following bills and resolutions[147] illustrate ongoing congressional efforts to address, reinterpret, or propose changes to the natural-born citizen requirement:

H.J. Res. 59[148] (108th Congress) — "President and Vice President Eligibility for Office." Sponsored by Rep. Vic Snyder (D), introduced June 11, 2003.

H.J. Res. 67[149] (108th Congress), Proposing an amendment to permit persons who are not natural-born citizens, but who have been citizens for at least 20 years, to be eligible for President. Sponsored by Rep. John Conyers Jr. (D), introduced September 3, 2003.

S. 2128[150] (108th Congress), "Natural-born Citizen Act." Sponsored by Sen. Don Nickles (R), introduced February 25, 2005.

146 U.S. Const. art. V.

147 See Congressional Research Service and Congress.gov legislative records for proposed constitutional amendments and resolutions concerning presidential eligibility.

148 https://www.govtrack.us/congress/bills/108/hjres59

149 https://www.congress.gov/bill/108th-congress/house-joint-resolution/67

150 https://www.congress.gov/member/donald-nickles/N000102

H.J. Res. 104[151] (108th Congress), Amendment proposal to make long-term citizens eligible for the presidency. Sponsored by Rep. Dana Rohrabacher (R), introduced September 15, 2004.

H.J. Res. 2[152] (109th Congress), Amendment proposal permitting non–natural-born citizens with 20 years' citizenship to serve as President. Sponsored by Rep. John Conyers Jr. (D), introduced January 4, 2005.

H.J. Res. 15[153] (109th Congress), Amendment proposal regarding presidential eligibility. Sponsored by Rep. Dana Rohrabacher (R), introduced February 1, 2005.

H.J. Res. 42[154] (109th Congress), Amendment proposal permitting long-term citizens to serve as President and Vice President. Sponsored by Rep. Vic Snyder (D), introduced April 14, 2005.

S. 2678[155] (110th Congress), "Children of Military Families Natural-born Citizen Act," seeks to clarify eligibility for children born abroad to U.S. citizen parents in military service. Sponsored by Sen. Claire McCaskill (D), with cosponsors including Sen. Hillary Clinton and Sen. Barack Obama.

S. Res. 511[156] (110th Congress), Senate resolution recognizing John Sidney McCain III as a natural-born citizen. Sponsored by Sen. Claire McCaskill (D), introduced April 30, 2008.

These measures reveal a persistent recognition in Congress that presidential eligibility raises constitutional questions that require formal clarification or amendment. The repeated introduction of proposed amendments rather than ordinary legislation reflects

---

151 https://www.congress.gov/bill/108th-congress/house-joint-resolution/104

152 https://www.congress.gov/bill/109th-congress/house-joint-resolution/2/text/ih

153 https://www.govinfo.gov/content/pkg/BILLS-109hjres15ih/pdf/BILLS-109hjres15ih.pdf

154 https://www.congress.gov/bill/109th-congress/house-joint-resolution/42

155 https://www.congress.gov/bill/110th-congress/senate-bill/2678/text#:~:text=Introduced%20in%20Senate%20(02/28,Share%20This

156 https://www.congress.gov/bill/110th-congress/senate-resolution/511/text

an understanding that the natural-born-citizen requirement is embedded in the Constitution itself and cannot be altered by statute alone.

Why would Congress repeatedly propose constitutional amendments if the meaning of the natural-born citizen requirement were already settled?

Having traced the intellectual foundations, we now turn to how these principles were evaluated in modern institutions.

As this book approached its final stages of editing, the issue of citizenship and allegiance unexpectedly returned to national attention. On April 1, 2026, the United States Supreme Court heard oral arguments in a case addressing birthright citizenship and the meaning of the Fourteenth Amendment's phrase "subject to the jurisdiction thereof." During the arguments, the concept of domicile emerged repeatedly as attorneys and justices struggled to define the scope of citizenship and political allegiance.

The discussion revealed an unusual and striking reality: although domicile was being invoked as a key legal concept, there appeared to be little agreement among the parties or the Court regarding its precise meaning. The arguments repeatedly returned to whether citizenship depended merely on physical presence within the United States, or whether a more permanent political attachment, often described as domicile, was required.

This uncertainty is remarkable because the concept of domicile was clearly defined in the eighteenth-century legal framework familiar to the Founding generation, most notably in Emmerich de Vattel's *Law of Nations*, a work repeatedly cited throughout this study and widely circulated among the Founders.

Unlike modern debates, Vattel addressed domicile directly and with precision.

In Book I, Chapter 19, Vattel distinguishes between citizens, inhabitants, and foreigners, explaining that residence alone does not confer citizenship. He writes:

"The inhabitants, as distinguished from citizens, are foreigners who are permitted to settle and stay in the country. Bound to the society by their residence, they are subject to the laws of the state while they reside in it, but they do not participate in all the rights of citizens."

This passage makes a critical distinction. A person may reside within a country and be subject to its laws, yet still not be a citizen. Residence, therefore, is not synonymous with political membership.

Vattel then turns directly to the concept of domicile, explaining that domicile requires more than mere physical presence. He explains that domicile is established only when a person fixes his habitation in a place with the intention of remaining there permanently. Temporary residence, even lawful residence, does not create domicile.

This distinction was fundamental to eighteenth-century legal thought. Under Vattel's framework:

- Residence does not equal citizenship
- Presence does not equal allegiance
- Settlement does not equal political membership
- Domicile requires permanent attachment and intention

These distinctions were well understood in the law of nations and formed part of the intellectual environment in which the Founders operated.

The concept of domicile is closely tied to allegiance. Vattel's framework assumes that citizenship reflects a durable political bond between the individual and the sovereign. That bond arises not merely from geography, but from permanent attachment and political membership within a civil society.

This understanding aligns with earlier discussions in this book concerning allegiance and natural-born citizenship. If citizenship reflects political membership, and domicile reflects permanent attachment, then domicile becomes a critical component in understanding citizenship itself.

The relevance of this concept becomes even more striking when viewed in light of the Supreme Court's April 1, 2026, arguments. During those proceedings, the term "domicile" repeatedly surfaced as attorneys and justices sought to determine whether citizenship depends solely on birth within the territory or whether political allegiance and permanent attachment must also be considered.

Yet the uncertainty displayed during those arguments stands in contrast to the clarity found in Vattel's work, a source known to the Founders, circulated among colonial leaders, consulted by Congress, and referenced by courts throughout American history.

Indeed, as shown earlier, American courts during the Reconstruction era continued to cite Vattel in connection with citizenship and domicile, alongside authorities such as Kent and Story. This demonstrates that the concept of domicile was not an obscure philosophical idea, but a recognized legal principle within American jurisprudence.

That this concept reappeared in a Supreme Court argument in April 2026, more than two centuries after the Founding, underscores the continuing relevance of the law-of-nations framework familiar to the Founders.

The timing of this Supreme Court decision and my book release is extremely noteworthy. Books addressing constitutional interpretation typically require years, often decades, to research, write, edit, and publish. Yet this volume, nearing publication, now finds itself referencing a Supreme Court argument that occurred less than 2 months before its release.

This convergence is unusual. The historical inquiry traced throughout this work, examining natural law, allegiance, citizenship, and the law of nations, unexpectedly intersects with a contemporary constitutional debate unfolding in real time.

On the publication date of this book, the Court had yet to issue its decision, arguments presented on April 1, 2026, demonstrate that the meanings of citizenship and allegiance remain unsettled in modern legal discourse. The fact that the Founding generation operated within a framework that clearly addressed these concepts, including domicile, underscores the value of returning to the sources that shaped their understanding.

Vattel did not leave the concept undefined. He articulated a clear distinction between residence and citizenship, between presence and allegiance, and between temporary settlement and permanent political attachment.

- The Founders read Vattel.
- They cited Vattel.
- They circulated Vattel.
- They taught Vattel in early American law schools.
- Congress acquired Vattel for official use.
- Courts cited Vattel when addressing citizenship and domicile.

When modern courts struggle to define domicile, the Founding-era sources provide clarity.

The concept was not invented recently.

It was understood at the founding.

And, as the Supreme Court now revisits questions of citizenship and allegiance, the law-of-nations framework familiar to the Founders, including Vattel's definition of domicile, once again becomes relevant to understanding the constitutional language they adopted.

IV

The Shift in Interpretation

How legal doctrine and public understanding diverged from earlier principles

IV

The Shift in Interpretation

How legal doctrine and public understanding diverged from earlier principles

When news emerged that the Supreme Court would hear cases on executive actions related to birthright citizenship, I felt a renewed urgency to gather all my evidence and complete my work. The national conversation once again turned toward questions that had occupied my research for many years, and this book is essential.

I also wish to acknowledge the role of certain political developments in bringing renewed attention to these issues. Executive actions and legal challenges have placed questions of citizenship before the courts once more, ensuring that they cannot be ignored.

Whatever conclusions readers ultimately draw, I hope that this chapter provides insight into why I undertook this journey and why I felt compelled to document both the historical record and my personal experience along the way.

At this point in the narrative, it becomes necessary to return briefly to the controversy surrounding Barack Obama's presidential eligibility. The purpose of revisiting that constitutional question is not to single out any individual for criticism, nor to re-litigate the political disputes of a past election. Rather, the question provides a modern example of how the constitutional requirement of a 'natural-born Citizen' has been interpreted over the past few decades.

The central concern addressed in this chapter is not the personal status of any candidate, but the broader shift in constitutional interpretation that occurred during that period. Historically, discussions of allegiance and citizenship in the Founding era often emphasized birth within the political community and the absence of foreign allegiance. In contemporary debates, however, the prevailing interpretation increasingly treats birth within the territorial United States as sufficient by itself, regardless of parental allegiance or legal status. If that interpretation is correct, it would apply broadly across the political spectrum. It could affect the eligibility analysis of numerous modern political figures, including individuals such as Barack Obama, Marco Rubio, Kamala Harris, Nikki Haley, and others whose family histories have been discussed in public commentary. The purpose of examining these debates is therefore not partisan, but constitutional, to understand how the meaning of the presidential eligibility clause has evolved and why that shift raises questions about how the Framers' requirement should be understood today.

When the Obama eligibility issue first arose, public discussion focused primarily on the question of where he was born. Some commentators asserted that he was born in Kenya and argued that this would affect his eligibility, while others maintained that he had been born in Hawaii.

As I began researching the issue, I sought to locate contemporary records describing how Obama's birthplace had been represented during the early years of his political career.

Because online content can be edited or removed after publication, researchers often rely on archival tools that preserve earlier versions of web pages. One such resource is the Internet Archive, commonly known as the Wayback Machine, located at https://web.archive.org. This digital archive captures snapshots of websites across time, allowing users to view how webpages appeared on specific dates. By examining these archived records, it becomes possible to compare earlier versions of web pages with later revisions and document how online information has changed.

To demonstrate how the website works, I searched for "whitehouse.gov."[157] The interactive calendar below displays archived captures, with a graph at the top showing the website activity over time. By selecting a date, you can view the exact appearance of the website on that day.

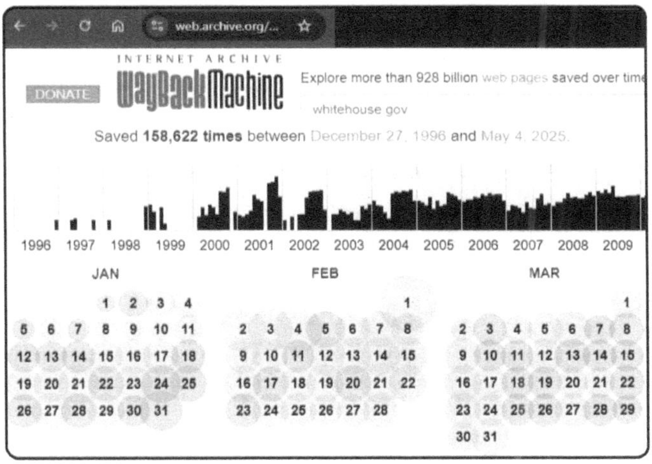

When clicking a highlighted date, the archived version of the webpage appears. As shown in the figure below, the top image shows the website on December 27, 1996 — the first day it was archived — as a simple, basic page, illustrating how the archive preserves historical snapshots of web content.

The website remained largely unchanged until October 23, 1997, and as you can see the difference in the bottom image, the archived record shows a significant update to its design and content.

157 Wayback Machine, "whitehouse.gov" results page https://web.archive.org/web/*/http://www.whitehouse.gov/

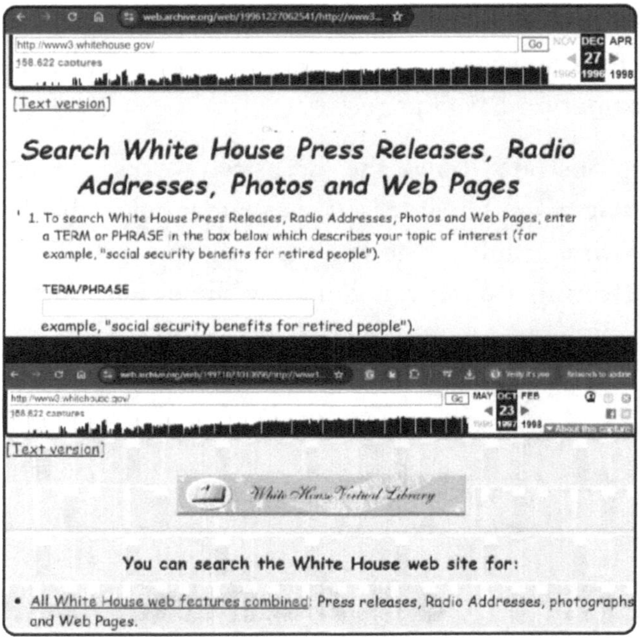

Now that you can see how the Wayback Machine tracks page edits and preserves earlier versions of webpages, including changes over time, the pattern becomes harder to ignore.

I want to demonstrate how a number of articles I collected appeared to have been edited or removed altogether. The first example I encountered was a Kenyan website that, at the time, stated that Barack Obama was born there.

The archived article was originally captured on May 18, 2010. At that time, the page included a striking statement:

"Kisumu is a relatively ordinary Kenyan city, or at least it would be if it weren't for the fact that U.S. President Barack Obama was born here."[158]

158 "Kenya World Guide" page (Kisumu) May 18, 2010, https://web.archive.org/web/20100518*/http://www.kenya.world-guides.com/kenya_districts.html

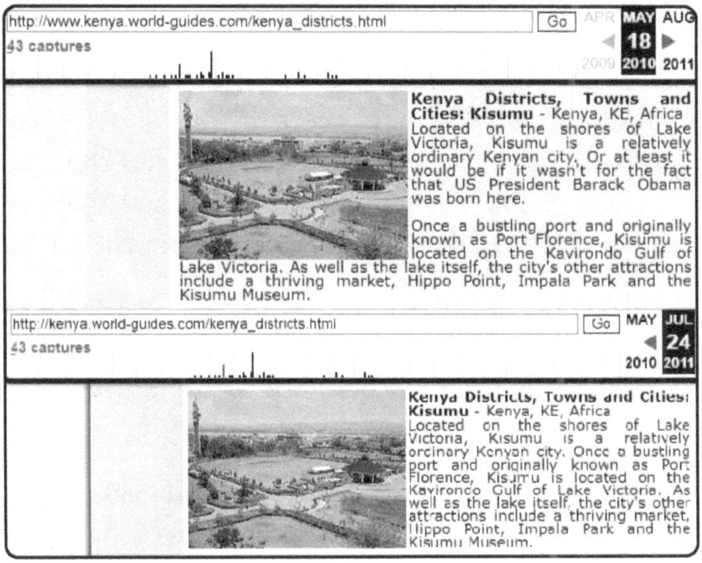

The highlighted yellow box in the top-left of the top image shows little to no internet traffic. Nearly a year later, on July 21, 2011,[159] the archived record shows the page still containing the same language. However, the traffic graph indicates a noticeable spike in page views, suggesting that public attention to the page had increased.

Then, just three days later,[160] as you can see in the bottom image, the archived version reveals a change. The reference to Obama being born in Kisumu had been removed. No explanation appears on the site, and no editorial note accompanies the revision. The statement simply disappears from the public record.

This sequence, original publication, heightened traffic, and subsequent removal, highlights the importance of archival tools in tracking how information evolves online.

Whether the edit resulted from routine correction, outside

159 Ibid., same page archived July 21, 2011, https://web.archive.org/web/20110721*/http://www.kenya.world-guides.com/kenya_districts.html

160 Ibid., capture list for the same page (showing subsequent revisions), accessed February 22, 2026, https://web.archive.org/web/*/http://www.kenya.world-guides.com/kenya_districts.html

inquiry, or internal review is not stated. What can be confirmed is that the archived timeline documents the presence of the statement and its later deletion, allowing readers to examine the sequence of events for themselves. Without preserved snapshots, such changes would be difficult to detect, and earlier versions of the record could easily be forgotten. The Kisumu people knew, and they wanted the world to know that President Obama came from their town.

On May 17, 2012, Breitbart.com reported on a 1991 promotional booklet produced by Obama's literary agency, Acton & Dystel,[161] which was created to promote his proposed book *Journeys in Black and White*, a manuscript he later abandoned.

The booklet includes biographies of the agency principals, Edward J. Acton and Jane Dystel, as well as a list of the firm's represented authors. Literary agencies typically rely on author-provided biographical information when preparing promotional materials, consistent with submission guidelines requesting authors to supply background details.

Within the booklet, Obama's author biography states that he "was born in Kenya and raised in Indonesia and Hawaii."[162]

Because this statement appears in a professional publishing brochure prepared for industry circulation, it provides an example of how Obama's background was described in contemporaneous materials.

This was not an isolated reference; it was one of many instances in which Obama was described as Kenyan-born, suggesting a broader pattern rather than a singular editorial mistake. The existence of this booklet raises further questions about how Obama's birthplace was represented and how those representations evolved over time.

---

161 Joel B. Pollak, "The Vetting: Barack Obama Literary Agent in 1991 Booklet Said 'Born in Kenya,'" Breitbart, May 17, 2012, https://www.breitbart.com/politics/2012/05/17/the-vetting-barack-obama-literary-agent-1991-born-in-kenya-raised-indonesia-hawaii/

162 Acton & Dystel, promotional booklet for proposed manuscript Journeys in Black and White (1991), excerpt reproduced in Pollak, "The Vetting: Barack Obama Literary Agent in 1991 Booklet Said, 'Born in Kenya.'"

Breitbart's coverage of the booklet can be found at Breitbart.com.[163]

Many articles I located over the years referred to Barack Obama as "Kenyan-born." Using the Wayback Machine, these references can be traced, compared, and examined to see how descriptions changed over time or were later removed.

In 2012, I compiled a video documenting these sources, including screenshots and web addresses to preserve the record.[164]

For readers approaching this material with skepticism, the purpose of presenting these records is not to suggest that any single item is dispositive, but to allow the cumulative record to be examined in its entirety. By considering the documents together, one can better evaluate how the issue was framed, contested, and interpreted over time.

An early headline from a 2004 article in the Sunday Standard read: "Kenyan-born Obama all set for US Senate."[165]

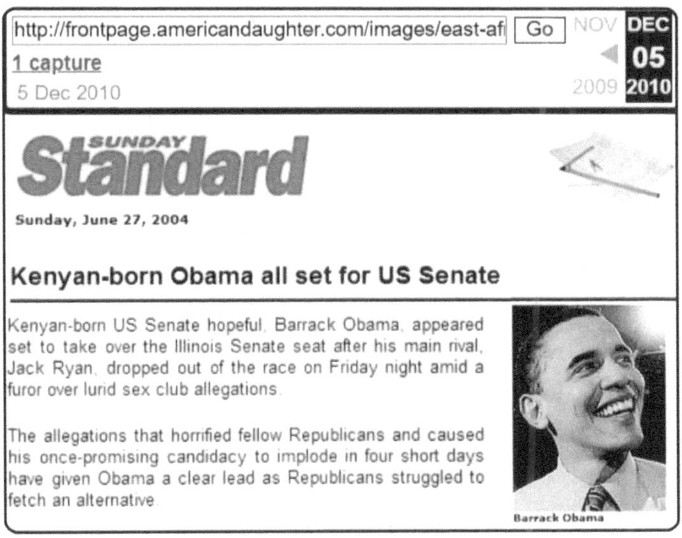

http://frontpage.americandaughter.com/images/east-af Go NOV DEC 05 2009 2010
1 capture
5 Dec 2010

SUNDAY Standard

Sunday, June 27, 2004

Kenyan-born Obama all set for US Senate

Kenyan-born US Senate hopeful, Barrack Obama, appeared set to take over the Illinois Senate seat after his main rival, Jack Ryan, dropped out of the race on Friday night amid a furor over lurid sex club allegations.

The allegations that horrified fellow Republicans and caused his once-promising candidacy to implode in four short days have given Obama a clear lead as Republicans struggled to fetch an alternative.

Barrack Obama

---

163 https://www.breitbart.com/politics/2012/05/17/the-vetting-barack-obama-literary-agent-1991-born-in-kenya-raised-indonesia-hawaii/

164 Obama literary agent claims Obama was Kenyan-born https://youtu.be/T1grt5uehak?si=AyiE73Zz7BHtFgjL

165 https://web.archive.org/web/20101205064925/http://frontpage.americandaughter.com/images/east-african-standard.jpg

Similar descriptions appeared across multiple publications in the years that followed.

During Senator Obama's 2006 visit to Kenya, where he and Michelle Obama publicly took an HIV test, public remarks referenced Kenya as his "home country."

In a 2008 speech, Michelle Obama stated that during their trip to "his home country in Kenya," they took a public HIV test,[166] reflecting how the narrative was framed publicly at the time. You can see the original video of the 2006 HIV test in Kenya on YouTube.[167]

Then, in 2008, Michelle Obama spoke at an LGBT delegate luncheon, sponsored by Barney Frank, Tammy Baldwin, the Victory Fund, and the Human Rights Campaign. At the 13:48 mark in the video, Michelle says:

"Barack has led by example; when we took our trip to Africa and visited his home country in Kenya, uh, we took a public HIV test."[168]

Archived articles from February 2008 reported: "As Kenyan-born US Senator Barack Obama jets into Kenya,"[169] while another noted that Ugandans had formed a support group for "Kenyan-born senator Barack Obama."[170] Headlines such as "KENYAN-BORN OBAMA MAKES HISTORY!"[171] appeared in African news coverage during the presidential campaign.

Additional reports from Nigerian, Turkish, and pan-African outlets similarly described Obama as Kenyan-born or as having ties to Kenya through citizenship or origin. Even U.S. reporting on African political perspectives referenced stories involving "Kenyan-born Sen. Barack Obama."

---

166 https://obamawhitehouse.archives.gov/blog/2011/12/01/archives-president-obama-says-get-tested

167 https://youtu.be/RNuA_jt0Od8

168 https://www.youtube.com/watch?v=NOc9cROLbK8

169 https://web.archive.org/web/20080214051127/http://www.africa-ata.org/ug_newsletter.htm

170 https://allafrica.com/stories/200802180051.html

171 http://www.usafricaonline.com/news.html

An article from The Nigerian Observer in 2008 states, "The Kenyan-born Senator will, however, face a stiff competition from his Republican counterpart, John McCain..."[172]

In a 2008 article from the U.S.-based media outlet NPR, Ofeibea Quist-Arcton refers to stories, including the presidential race of "Kenyan-born Sen. Barack Obama."[173]

An October 2008 archival record quotes commentary discussing "the oddity that a member of Kenya's Luo tribe (Barack Obama, a Kenyan citizen and Luo tribe member from birth) may become president of the United States."[174]

The collected references illustrate how widely and across diverse sources, Obama was described in terms linking him directly to Kenya. The recurrence of this language across independent outlets demonstrates that such descriptions circulated broadly in public discourse during the years surrounding his rise in national politics.

During the 2008 presidential campaign, reports surfaced that Barack Obama's passport records had been improperly accessed without authorization. According to contemporaneous news coverage, an employee of The Analysis Corporation, a government contractor, conducted unauthorized searches of Obama's passport file and those of other presidential candidates.[175]

At the time, John O. Brennan served as president and CEO of The Analysis Corporation. The incident drew national attention because passport records were protected under federal law, and unauthorized access raised questions about how and why the searches occurred during a presidential election cycle.

One of the individuals reported to have accessed the records was Lt. Quarles Harris Jr., who was cooperating with federal investigators

172 http://www.nigerianobservernews.com/4112008/4112008/news/news1.html

173 http://www.npr.org/templates/story/story.php?storyId=95550177

174 https://archive.org/details/OtunnuOnLuoTribeMemberBeingElectedPresidentOct.252008

175 Washington Times, "Key witness in passport fraud case fatally shot," April 19, 2008.

regarding the breach. In April 2008, Harris was found shot in the head outside a church in Washington, D.C. Authorities ruled the death a homicide, and the case remains unsolved.

The episode became part of the broader controversy surrounding the handling of records and information during the campaign. In later years, John Brennan would serve as Director of the Central Intelligence Agency.

Contemporary reporting on the incident can be found online.[176]

In 1967, when Barack Obama was six years old, his mother moved with him to Indonesia to live with her new husband, Lolo Soetoro. During this period, Obama attended school in Jakarta, and records from that time identify him under the name Barry Soetoro.[177]

These Indonesian school records list his citizenship as Indonesian and his religion as Islam. The documents also reflect his integration into Indonesian civil life during his years living there.

These records are cited here because questions of citizenship and allegiance are central to the constitutional discussion throughout this work.

The full Indonesian school record is reproduced below.

---

176 Audrey Hudson, "Key Witness in Passport Fraud Case Fatally Shot," Washington Times, April 19, 2008, https://www.washingtontimes.com/news/2008/apr/19/key-witness-in-passport-fraud-case-fatally-shot/

177 Indonesian school registration records reported during the 2008 presidential campaign.

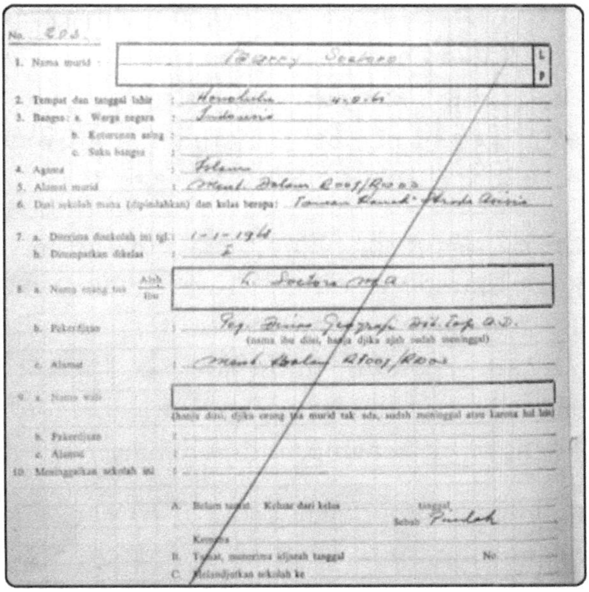

No. 203

1. Nama murid : Barry Soetoro — L / P

2. Tempat dan tanggal lahir : Honolulu 4.8.61

3. Bangsa : a. Warga negara : Indonesia

b. Keturunan asing :

c. Suku bangsa :

4. Agama : Islam

5. Alamat murid :

6. Dari sekolah mana (dipindahkan) dan kelas berapa :

7. a. Diterima disekolah ini tgl. :

b. Ditempatkan dikelas :

8. a. Nama orang tua Ajah / Ibu : L. Soetoro

b. Pekerdjaan :

(nama ibu diisi, hanja djika ajah sudah meninggal)

c. Alamat :

9. a. Nama wali :

(hanja diisi, djika orang tua murid tak ada, sudah meninggal atau karena hal lain)

b. Pekerdjaan :

c. Alamat :

10. Meninggalkan sekolah ini :

A. Belum tamat. Keluar dari kelas ... tanggal ... Sebab Pindah

Kemana

B. Tamat, menerima idjazah tanggal ... No.

C. Melandjutkan sekolah ke

These records became part of public discussion during the 2008 presidential campaign, when questions about Obama's early life were widely reported. That same year, the television program Inside Edition produced a documentary segment tracing Obama's childhood in Indonesia. The program's research took reporters to the schools he attended, where they reviewed local records.

Two segments aired, one on May 5, 2008,[178] and another on May 6, 2008.[179] The earlier segment included footage referencing the school records that identified him as Barry Soetoro. The later segment did not include the same material.

The May 5, 2008, episode can be viewed on YouTube, as can the May 6, 2008, episode.

Because media coverage and online content can change over time, copies and references preserved during that period remain important for historical review.

178 Inside Edition segment (May 5, 2008) posted to YouTube, https://www.youtube.com/watch?v=TwEd3i1Dymo&t=62s

179 Inside Edition segment (May 6, 2008) posted to YouTube, https://www.youtube.com/watch?v=y1CEeEFOsSg

An Indonesia Matters article published in 2008, refers to Obama using the name Barry Soetoro, the name associated with his time in Indonesia following his mother's marriage to Lolo Soetoro. The article also references his parentage, noting that he was born to Ann Dunham and Barack Hussein Obama Sr.

The continued use of the name Barry Soetoro in contemporary reporting raises questions about how Obama was identified internationally at different points in his life, particularly regarding his childhood and schooling in Indonesia. These references are presented here as part of the broader historical record surrounding questions of identity, citizenship, and public narrative.

As with other contemporaneous sources, the significance lies not in any single article but in the pattern of references across multiple outlets during the period. Examining these materials helps illustrate how Obama's background was described in various contexts prior to and during his rise to national prominence.

Moving forward in the timeline, I examined records from the Kenyan Parliament, which maintains an official transcript archive known as the Plenary Hansard. The Hansard is equivalent to the United States Congressional Record and preserves the official proceedings and statements made during parliamentary sessions.[180]

As I began reviewing the Hansard minutes, I encountered statements that I considered significant to the historical record. The following excerpt is taken from a House meeting held on December 5, 2008.[181]

The text reads as follows:

"President-elect, Mr. Obama, is a son of the soil of this country. Every other country on this continent is celebrating Obama's win. It is only proper and fitting that the country from which he originates

---

180 Parliament of Kenya, Hansard Department, official parliamentary transcript archive, https://www.parliament.go.ke/the-senate/hansard-department

181 Parliament of Kenya, National Assembly Hansard, December 5, 2008 session transcript.

should show the same excitement, pomp, and color."[182]

> November 5, 2008 PARLIAMENTARY DEBATES 3277
>
> **POINT OF ORDER**
>
> HOUSE SHOULD ADJOURN TO DISCUSS
> ELECTION OF MR. BARRACK OBAMA
>
> **Ms. Odhiambo:** On a point of order, Mr. Deputy Speaker, Sir. It is not on this issue. I stand on a point of order under Standing Order No.20 to seek leave for adjournment of the House to discuss the American presidential election results.
>
> *(Applause)*
>
> Mr. Deputy Speaker, Sir, the President-elect, Mr. Obama, is a son of the soil of this country. Every other country in this continent is celebrating the Obama win. It is only proper and fitting that the country which he originates should show the same excitement, pomp and colour. I, therefore, seek leave of the House that we adjourn to discuss the issue.

Then again, on March 25, 2010, the Hansard contains another statement I considered significant. During parliamentary discussion, the following remark was entered into the official record:

"If America were living in a situation where it feared ethnicity and did not see itself as a multiparty state or nation, how could a young man born here in Kenya, who is not even a native American, become the President of America? It is because they did away with exclusion."[183]

> **March 25, 2010 PARLIAMENTARY DEBATES 643**
>
> **The Minister for Lands** (Mr. Orengo):
>
> The other thing that we are addressing through devolution is exclusion. What has made us suffer as a nation is exclusion. Once people feel excluded, even when you want to employ a policeman or constable or you want to build a dispensary, it must come from the centre. In the colonial days, these things were being done on the ground and they could give bursaries and build roads. I commend devolution. Those who fear devolution are living in the past. They are being guided by their ethnic consideration and objectives. They are living in the past. If America was living in a situation where they feared ethnicity and did not see itself as a multiparty state or nation, how could a young man born here in Kenya, who is not even a native American, become the President of America? It is because they did away with exclusion.

This entry, preserved in the official transcript of proceedings, reflects how the topic was discussed in the Kenyan Parliament at the time and provides additional context for the broader timeline

182 Kenya National Assembly, Parliamentary Debates (Hansard), Dec. 5, 2008. https://hansardna.parliament.go.ke/server/api/core/bitstreams/c777514d-743e-45e6-bc89-0262463660eb/content

183 Kenya National Assembly, Parliamentary Debates (Hansard), Mar. 25, 2010. https://hansardna.parliament.go.ke/server/api/core/bitstreams/c599fb0d-f27b-4047-ba86-4a5371744008/content

under examination.

We then have the transcript from a radio call between the Kenyan Ambassador to the United States, Peter Ogego, and WRIF's The Mike in the Morning Show in Detroit, Michigan.[184] The call can be heard on a YouTube video[185] with the relevant audio beginning around the five-minute mark:

The transcript reads as follows:

The Morning Show:

"Well, listen, we want to congratulate you on, uh, on uh, Barack Obama, uh, as our new president, and uh, you must be very proud."

Ambassador Peter Ogego:

"We are, really are. We are so proud of the US, uh, for having, uh, uh made history as well."

The Morning Show:

"Hey, one more, one more quick question. Um, Obama, President-elect Obama's birthplace over in Kenya, is that gonna be a national, uh, spot to visit, where he was born?"

Ambassador Peter Ogego:

"It's um, already uh, an attraction, uh his, his, his uh, paternal grandmother is still alive and, uh, uh…"

The Morning Show:

"But his, his birthplace will be, they'll put up a marker there?"

Ambassador Peter Ogego:

"They do. Uh, it's already well known. Uh, yeah."

Can so many media outlets be mistaken about where Obama

---

184 Interview with Ambassador Peter Ogego, WRIF "Mike in the Morning Show," archived recording.

185 "Kenyan Ambassador Peter Ogego interview," WRIF "Mike in the Morning Show," audio recording, https://www.youtube.com/watch?v=T1grt5uehak&t=112s

was born? The question naturally arises: why did statements like these appear repeatedly in public discourse while the issue remained contested in the United States?

As public attention intensified, Americans increasingly demanded documentary clarification regarding Obama's birthplace. On June 14, 2008, Obama's campaign website released a Certification of Live Birth, a document distinct from a long-form birth certificate, which was presented as evidence addressing those concerns.

Obama's "Fight the Smears" website claimed that it was false to question whether he was a natural-born citizen and cited the 14th Amendment as proof of his eligibility.[186] The site stated that Senator Obama was born in Hawaii in 1961 and therefore became a citizen at birth under the citizenship clause.

However, this claim itself raises a deeper constitutional question. The phrase "subject to the jurisdiction thereof," as discussed throughout this work, has historically been understood to mean complete political allegiance, not subject to any foreign power. At the time of Obama's birth, his father was a British subject governed by the British Nationality Act of 1948, raising questions about whether Obama was born with divided allegiance.

The media widely circulated the Certification of Live Birth (COLB), presenting it as proof that the matter was settled. Yet many Americans pointed out that a COLB differs from a long-form birth certificate and argued that possession of a COLB implies that an original birth record exists.

Because the long-form birth certificate was not immediately released, public debate quickly shifted to a new question: "Where is the birth certificate?" This question persisted for years and became a national controversy. The issue drew widespread attention, including the publication of Jerome Corsi's book *Where's the Birth*

186 Barack Obama campaign, "Fight the Smears: The Truth About Barack's Birth Certificate," archived campaign webpage, https://web.archive.org/web/20080614/http://my.barackobama.com/page/invite/birthcert (accessed February 22, 2026).

Certificate?[187], which examined the dispute and the surrounding evidence.

My research uncovered several Obama birth certificates. I still have no way of determining whether these documents are authentic or fabricated, but they contain registration numbers and official markings that could potentially be examined or verified. For that reason, they are referenced here as potential evidence that warrants further scrutiny.

The first birth certificate I came across was from Coast Province General Hospital[188] in Mombasa, Kenya and was posted by his brother in Kenya. It bears what appears to be an official stamp in the upper left corner, a seal in the lower right, and even a baby footprint near the bottom, features typically associated with hospital birth records.

I then encountered a second Kenyan birth certificate[189] listing the registration district as Mombasa, Kenya, while identifying the birth hospital as King George VI Hospital in Nairobi. This creates the impression that Obama may have been born at the Coast Province General Hospital in Mombasa and later associated with King George VI Hospital in Nairobi, suggesting a sequence of events that could explain the differing records.

Because these documents raise questions but have not been definitively authenticated, they are presented here as part of the broader record of claim and materials that have circulated over the years. Their existence illustrates the extent of the controversy and the ongoing uncertainty surrounding the issue.

An example of how Obama's background was described in contemporary reporting appeared in a 2006 article in The Honolulu Advertiser. In discussing Illinois congressional candidate Tammy

---

187 Jerome R. Corsi, Where's the Birth Certificate? The Case That Barack Obama Is Not Eligible to Be President (Washington, DC: WND Books, 2011).

188 https://www.thesun.co.uk/news/3063752/barack-obamas-brother-posts-document-he-claims-is-ex-presidents-kenyan-birth-certificate/

189 https://freeimage.host/i/qEBHsI4

Duckworth, the article noted that Duckworth and Barack Obama shared what it called a "kama'aina connection," referring to their ties to Hawai'i. The article stated that both individuals had been born outside the United States, Obama in Indonesia and Duckworth in Thailand, and that both later attended high school in Honolulu. The report described Obama as a graduate of Punahou School who had been raised in Hawai'i.[190]

Not to mention the widespread public reaction that followed, across the country, citizens began expressing their concerns through visible public demonstrations, including billboards, roadside signs, and grassroots campaigns calling attention to the unresolved questions surrounding presidential eligibility.

Slogans such as "Where's the Birth Certificate?" appeared on highways,[191] in neighborhoods, and along major travel routes, reflecting a growing sentiment among many Americans that transparency on the issue was necessary. These displays illustrate that the controversy was not confined to courtrooms or political debate but had entered the broader public consciousness as a matter of national discussion.

In January 2009, Bishop Ron McRae of the Anabaptist Church Worldwide participated in a recorded telephone call with Reverend Kweli Shuhubia, a Kenyan evangelical minister who was present at Sarah Obama's residence in Kogelo, Kenya. Reverend Shuhubia placed the call from the home and put the conversation on speakerphone. Bishop McRae states that permission to record the interview was obtained from those present.

Because Sarah Obama spoke Swahili, her grandson served as translator during the conversation. During the call, Bishop McRae asked where Barack Obama was born. According to the translation provided at the time, Sarah Obama responded that he was born in

190 The Honolulu Advertiser, Jan. 8, 2006, https://web.archive.org/web/20060207151627/https://the.honoluluadvertiser.com/article/2006/Jan/08/ln/FP601080334.html

191 "Where's the Birth Certificate?" Billboards https://www.zocalopublicsquare.org/we-are-all-birthers-now/

Kenya and indicated that she was present at the birth.

A recording of this call is publicly available and can be heard beginning at approximately 5:40 in the YouTube video.[192]

The recording is presented as contemporaneous testimonial evidence for the reader's consideration.

Throughout my research, I connected with others across the country who were actively pursuing legal challenges to President Obama's eligibility. One of those individuals was Dr. Orly Taitz, a California dentist and attorney. We met several times in Washington, D.C., where we attended rallies and discussed the growing body of evidence surrounding the issue.

In September 2009, Dr. Taitz filed suit in federal court in Georgia on behalf of Army Captain Connie Rhodes, who sought to avoid deployment to Iraq on the grounds that questions remained regarding President Obama's eligibility. The court denied Captain Rhodes' request and warned Dr. Taitz against filing what it characterized as "frivolous" litigation on the matter.

Dr. Taitz subsequently filed additional pleadings. In response, U.S. District Judge Clay Land imposed a $20,000 sanction,[193] stating that she had used the court system to advance claims challenging President Obama's citizenship that the court deemed without merit.

In August 2010, the Supreme Court declined to intervene, leaving the sanction in place.

To many observers, these rulings became emblematic of the broader judicial response to (and resistance against) attempts to litigate questions surrounding presidential eligibility, reinforcing the perception among critics that courts were unwilling to allow evidentiary exploration of the issue.

192 Recording described as a 2009 telephone conversation with Sarah Obama, Bishop Ron McRae and Rev. Kweli Shuhubia, YouTube video https://youtu.be/CY6bPYKLjNw

193 *Rhodes v. MacDonald,* U.S. District Court (M.D. Ga. 2009). Judge Fines Birther Attorney $20,000," Courthouse News Service, October 13, 2009, https://www.courthousenews.com/judge-fines-birther-attorney-20000/

From my perspective, the sanctions sent a chilling message: that raising constitutional questions in court could come at significant personal and professional cost.

In March 2010, an Army physician with 18 years of active-duty service, Lieutenant Colonel Terry Lakin, refused orders to deploy to Afghanistan, stating that he would not comply until President Obama produced documentation proving he was a natural-born citizen and therefore eligible to serve as Commander in Chief.

Lieutenant Colonel Lakin's actions led to a court-martial proceeding[194] later that year. In December 2010, I attended portions of the court-martial along with dozens of supporters who believed the underlying constitutional questions deserved to be examined.

At trial, Lieutenant Colonel Lakin was convicted on multiple counts, including four counts of disobeying orders and one count of missing movement. Following his conviction, he was dismissed from service, forfeited pay and allowances, and was sentenced to six months' confinement at the U.S. Disciplinary Barracks at Fort Leavenworth.

To many who followed the case, the outcome reinforced the view that service members raising constitutional concerns regarding presidential eligibility faced severe consequences without an opportunity to litigate the underlying issue in court.

Supporters, including myself, responded by contacting members of Congress, writing letters to the White House, engaging the media, and pursuing every available avenue to advocate for Lieutenant Colonel Lakin.

For those who believed the issue remained unresolved, the case became a defining moment — symbolizing both the depth of conviction among challengers and the institutional resistance they perceived.

---

194 *United States v. Lakin,* court-martial proceedings (2010). https://www.scribd.com/document/61479490/LTC-TERRENCE-LAKIN-TRANSCRIPT-OF-RECORD-PROCEEDINGS-OF-A-GENERAL-COURT-MARTIAL-LAKIN-Transcript-Redacted-Copy

Four months after the court-martial of Lieutenant Colonel Lakin, while he was still serving his sentence, events took a significant turn regarding the issue of President Obama's birth records.

On April 22, 2011, the law firm Perkins Coie, acting on behalf of President Barack Obama, submitted a formal request to the Hawaii Department of Health seeking certified copies of his original Certificate of Live Birth. The correspondence from Perkins Coie[195] to Hawaii Health Director Loretta Fuddy outlines the request and confirms that Obama authorized his personal counsel to obtain certified copies of the records.

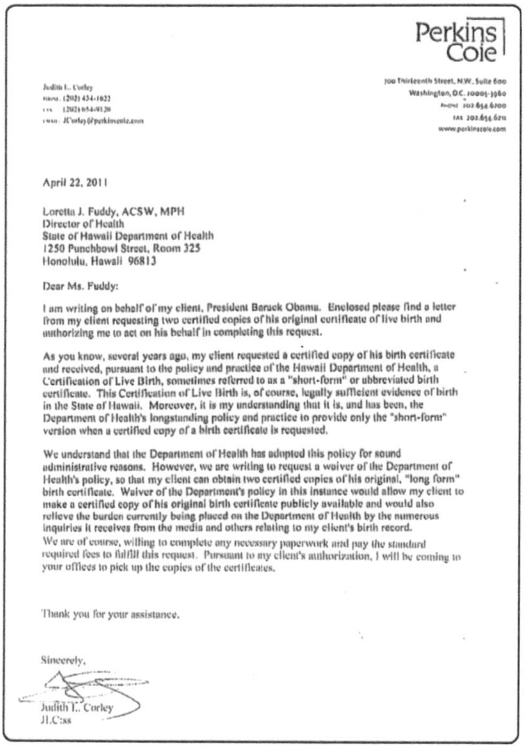

Perkins Coie

Judith L. Corley
Phone: (202) 434-1622
Fax: (202) 654-9120
Email: JCorley@perkinscoie.com

700 Thirteenth Street, N.W., Suite 600
Washington, D.C. 20005-3960
Phone: 202.654.6200
Fax: 202.654.6211
www.perkinscoie.com

April 22, 2011

Loretta J. Fuddy, ACSW, MPH
Director of Health
State of Hawaii Department of Health
1250 Punchbowl Street, Room 325
Honolulu, Hawaii 96813

Dear Ms. Fuddy:

I am writing on behalf of my client, President Barack Obama. Enclosed please find a letter from my client requesting two certified copies of his original certificate of live birth and authorizing me to act on his behalf in completing this request.

As you know, several years ago, my client requested a certified copy of his birth certificate and received, pursuant to the policy and practice of the Hawaii Department of Health, a Certification of Live Birth, sometimes referred to as a "short-form" or abbreviated birth certificate. This Certification of Live Birth is, of course, legally sufficient evidence of birth in the State of Hawaii. Moreover, it is my understanding that it is, and has been, the Department of Health's longstanding policy and practice to provide only the "short-form" version when a certified copy of a birth certificate is requested.

We understand that the Department of Health has adopted this policy for sound administrative reasons. However, we are writing to request a waiver of the Department of Health's policy, so that my client can obtain two certified copies of his original, "long form" birth certificate. Waiver of the Department's policy in this instance would allow my client to make a certified copy of his original birth certificate publicly available and would also relieve the burden currently being placed on the Department of Health by the numerous inquiries it receives from the media and others relating to my client's birth record.
We are of course, willing to complete any necessary paperwork and pay the standard required fees to fulfill this request. Pursuant to my client's authorization, I will be coming to your offices to pick up the copies of the certificates.

Thank you for your assistance.

Sincerely,

Judith L. Corley
JLC:ss

Accompanying the Perkins Coie letter was a separate written authorization, likewise dated April 22, 2011, signed by Barack Obama himself, requesting two certified copies of his original

195 Letter from Judith Corley, Perkins Coie LLP, to Loretta J. Fuddy at the Hawaii Department of Health, Apr. 22, 2011 https://obamawhitehouse.archives.gov/sites/default/files/rss_viewer/birth-certificate-correspondence.pdf

Certificate of Live Birth and authorizing counsel to act on his behalf.

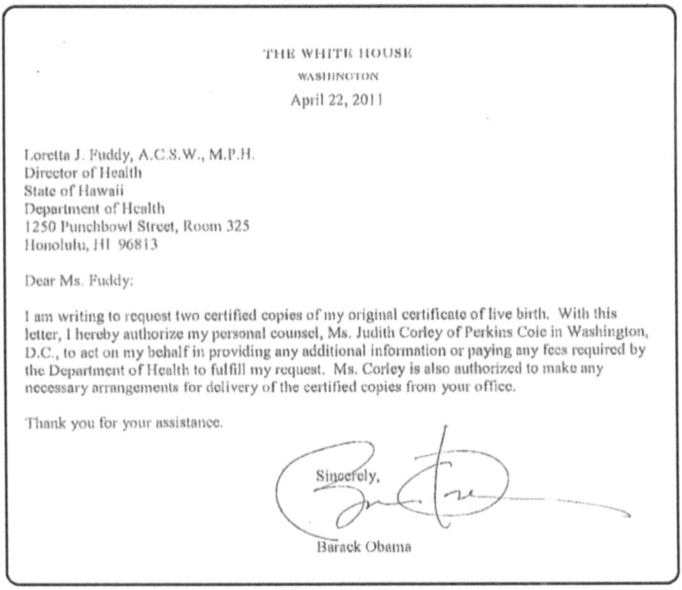

THE WHITE HOUSE
WASHINGTON
April 22, 2011

Loretta J. Fuddy, A.C.S.W., M.P.H.
Director of Health
State of Hawaii
Department of Health
1250 Punchbowl Street, Room 325
Honolulu, HI 96813

Dear Ms. Fuddy:

I am writing to request two certified copies of my original certificate of live birth. With this letter, I hereby authorize my personal counsel, Ms. Judith Corley of Perkins Coie in Washington, D.C., to act on my behalf in providing any additional information or paying any fees required by the Department of Health to fulfill my request. Ms. Corley is also authorized to make any necessary arrangements for delivery of the certified copies from your office.

Thank you for your assistance.

Sincerely,

Barack Obama

These documents demonstrate that the request for records was initiated through legal channels and handled directly between Obama's representatives and the Hawaii Department of Health.

If the name Perkins Coie sounds familiar, it is because the same law firm later became widely known for its role representing Hillary Clinton's presidential campaign and the Democratic National Committee, including hiring Fusion GPS for approximately $1.2 million to conduct opposition research. Fusion GPS, in turn, paid $168,000 to Christopher Steele's firm, Orbis Business Intelligence, to produce the dossier related to allegations of Russian interference. This connection has drawn attention from observers who note the firm's recurring involvement in high-profile political controversies.

Shortly thereafter, Hawaii officials issued public statements regarding the matter. A news release dated April 27, 2011,[196] from the office of Governor Neil Abercrombie and the Hawaii Department

196 News release, April 27, 2011. https://health.hawaii.gov/vitalrecords/files/2013/05/News_Release_Birth_Certificate_042711.pdf

of Health confirmed that certified copies of the long-form birth certificate had been provided to President Obama.

The release stated that Health Director Loretta Fuddy personally witnessed the copying of the original records and attested to their authenticity. The statement further explained that the Department followed established procedures and that the records confirmed Obama's birth in Honolulu, Hawaii.

Notably, the same release also references Obama's earlier 2008 request for a Certification of Live Birth, the short-form document that had previously been made public, confirming that both the short-form and the long-form records had been requested at different times.

These developments marked a pivotal moment in the public controversy, as the administration responded to ongoing requests for documentation. Yet disagreement persisted regarding the meaning, sufficiency, and legal significance of the birth records among supporters, critics, and constitutional commentators.

This transition was marked by a response dated April 25, 2011, from Loretta J. Fuddy, Director of Health for the State of Hawaii Department of Health, addressed to President Barack Obama regarding his request for certified copies of his original Certificate of Live Birth.[197]

In the letter, Director Fuddy states that she reviewed the request for two certified copies of the original Certificate of Live Birth and, in recognition of Obama's status as President of the United States, made an exception to departmental policy governing how such records are produced. She further states that she witnessed the copying of the certificate and attested to the authenticity of the copies, noting that a payment receipt was attached.

The letter also expresses hope that issuing the copies would end the numerous inquiries received by the Hawaii Department of

197 Hawaii Dept. of Health correspondence, Apr. 25, 2011. https://health.hawaii.gov/vitalrecords/files/2013/05/News_Release_Birth_Certificate_042711.pdf

Health regarding the document.

In April of 2011, after years of declining to release it, Barack Obama publicly released what was described as his long-form birth certificate. The release came just days before the eligibility case of *Drake v. Obama*[198] was scheduled to proceed, a case involving multiple plaintiffs, including former presidential candidate Alan Keyes and Wiley Drake, who had been a vice-presidential candidate in 2008.

According to multiple reports, the Ninth Circuit Court of Appeals was preparing to hear arguments related to the case. Then, on April 27, 2011, the White House posted a PDF copy of the long-form Certificate of Live Birth on its official website.[199]

A copy of the long-form birth certificate, as first posted on April 27, 2011, can be viewed via the archived White House link in footnotes.

The release of this document did not settle the controversy. Instead, it prompted further examination and raised additional questions among those who had been closely following the issue.

After Obama posted his birth certificate, another 1961 Hawaii birth certificate surfaced online. This document was shared by the mother of twins born one day after Obama. The Nordyke twins were born on August 5, 1961, the day after Obama, and their certificates are very intriguing.

The Nordyke certificate[200] appears on white paper. By contrast, Obama's certificate is printed on green security paper, raising questions about when that paper stock came into use. In addition, Susan Nordyke's certificate number is 10637, while Obama's is listed as 10641. If Obama had been born the day before, one might expect his certificate number to appear earlier in the sequence.

---

198 *Drake v. Obama*, 664 F.3d 774 (9th Cir. 2011).

199 The White House, "Certificate of Live Birth," April 27, 2011 https://web.archive.org/web/20110427171111/http://www.whitehouse.gov/sites/default/files/rss_viewer/birth-certificate-long-form.pdf

200 https://disillusionedpatriot.weebly.com/birth-certificate-number.html

These differences prompted further scrutiny among researchers examining document formats, numbering practices, and archival procedures for Hawaii birth records from 1961.

Following the release of the long-form birth certificate, the controversy did not end; it intensified. Questions regarding the document's authenticity continued to circulate. For the first time, it appeared that a federal court might permit evidence concerning presidential eligibility to be examined in earnest in *Drake v. Obama*. Public attention grew as the proceedings approached, with many closely watching to see whether long-standing questions would finally be addressed on the record.

Dr. Orly Taitz's case gained significant traction, drawing increasing coverage across social media and traditional outlets. C-SPAN was even scheduled to air the coverage[201] of Dr. Taitz's upcoming oral arguments, reflecting the heightened national interest in the litigation.

However, on May 1, 2011, the night before those arguments, President Obama announced to the nation[202] that Osama bin Laden had been killed, declaring that "justice has been done." The announcement dominated headlines and broadcast coverage for weeks.

The sequence of events is notable. Just as a federal case challenging presidential eligibility was poised to receive broader public attention, the national conversation shifted almost overnight. For observers tracking the litigation, the timing raised questions about whether the issue would ever receive sustained scrutiny in the public arena.

I did everything within my power to bring this evidence to the attention of those in positions of authority. I repeatedly sent

---

201 https://www.c-span.org/program/news-conference/drake-v-obama-oral-arguments/250888

202 U.S. Department of Defense, "President Barack Obama Announces the Death of Osama bin Laden," May 1, 2011, https://www.defense.gov/Multimedia/Photos/igphoto/2002009777/

documentation to media outlets across the country, hoping that someone would take the time to examine the material and investigate further.

I attended Tea Party rallies across Maryland, Pennsylvania, Washington, D.C., and Virginia, distributing research packets and speaking with anyone willing to listen. Believing that elected officials had a duty to review the information, I printed hundreds of evidence packets and began making regular trips to Capitol Hill.

I went from office to office, starting with representatives I believed might be willing to act. At each office, I asked a staff member for their business card and handed over the packet. I asked them to sign the card acknowledging receipt and agreeing to pass the materials along to the members of Congress. Week after week, I walked through the halls of Congress collecting signatures and documenting deliveries. Although I accumulated stacks of signed cards confirming receipt, no meaningful action followed.

In 2011, members of the Surprise Tea Party in Arizona requested that their local sheriff examine concerns that the birth certificate released by Barack Obama might be fraudulent. In August 2011, Sheriff Joe Arpaio responded to these requests by forming a volunteer investigative team, the Cold Case Posse, to review the authenticity of the document and related records.

Sheriff Arpaio initially stated that his goal was to determine whether the document was legitimate, with the hope that a thorough review would address public concerns and bring clarity to the issue. According to statements made during the investigation, however, the inquiry led the team to conclude that the document showed signs they believed were consistent with forgery.

There is a video in which Sheriff Arpaio discusses listening to his constituents and initiating the investigation into the birth certificate that had been posted online[203]

203 Joe Arpaio, "Sheriff Joe Arpaio Announces Investigation into Obama Birth Certificate," YouTube video, accessed September 19, 2011 https://www.youtube.com/watch?v=IqJP9cvODA8

On March 2, 2012, Sheriff Arpaio held a press conference[204]. announcing the findings of the Cold Case Posse's six-month preliminary investigation into the birth certificate. A recording of that press conference can be viewed on YouTube via the link in the footnote. I talk more about this investigation later in the chapter.

In 2013, I attended an IRS protest rally where I personally provided my research materials to Dan Bongino, who at the time was a former U.S. Secret Service agent and U.S. Senate candidate from Maryland. During our conversation, he expressed the view that Obama was not eligible but indicated that, in his opinion, nothing could be done to change the situation.

I also attended one of Chris Plante's "Politics & a Pint" events in Virginia, where I handed him a packet of evidence and asked that he review the material and consider discussing it publicly. Although he indicated he would look into it, no further action followed.

However, I later heard Chris Plante discuss the issue of Obama's birth certificate on air, noting that the certificate was released after a prolonged period of public controversy. In April 2011, Plante specifically referenced Lieutenant Colonel Terry Lakin and his imprisonment after Lakin requested proof of the president's eligibility.[205]

A recording of Chris Plante discussing the Obama birth certificate can be viewed via the link in the footnote.

These encounters reinforced my growing realization that, despite widespread awareness, few were willing to pursue the issue publicly.

While participating in these events, I met many members of the Tea Party movement. In 2011, I connected with a woman from the Alleghany Tea Party. In 2012, we jointly filed a petition against Barack Obama and the Maryland Board of Elections for allowing

204 Maricopa County Sheriff's Office, Cold Case Posse press conference, Mar. 2, 2012. https://www.youtube.com/watch?v=yerPzQ4doyU

205 "Chris Plante Discusses the Obama Birth Certificate," YouTube video, April 2011, https://www.youtube.com/watch?v=D4Y-79TcBMU

an ineligible candidate to appear on the ballot. Our case ultimately reached the United States Supreme Court; however, it was never heard on the merits and was denied on procedural grounds, including laches and a determination that review was not in the public interest.

By May 2013, questions surrounding the authenticity of the birth certificate were resurfacing in public discussion, with even mainstream media outlets covering developments related to Sheriff Joe Arpaio's investigation. Fox News anchor Bret Baier conducted a segment with Sheriff Arpaio to address allegations about the document's validity.

Meanwhile, the numerous lawsuits filed before the 2012 election continued to work their way through the courts. Nearly all were dismissed on procedural grounds and moved into various stages of appeal. For many observers, these developments reinforced the perception that the underlying constitutional questions had not been fully examined.

In late 2013, activists Mike Volin, Jeff Harrison, and Tom Pavich traveled to Washington, D.C., to present informational packets, often referred to as "Sheriff's Kits," summarizing findings from the Cold Case Posse investigation. They met with House Majority Leader Kevin McCarthy and distributed materials to multiple members of Congress. Contemporary reporting, including coverage by CNN, documented the meeting and the activists' efforts to bring their concerns before federal officials.

As the birth certificate controversy grew, public attention expanded beyond the courts and increasingly focused on Hawaii officials. Eligibility challenges continued to be filed, and the Hawaii Department of Health reportedly adopted new procedures to manage an overwhelming volume of inquiries concerning the certificate. In particular, attention centered on the department's director, Loretta Fuddy, who oversaw the agency during the period when President Obama's birth records were requested and certified.

On December 11, 2013, Director Fuddy died following the

crash of a small commuter aircraft into the waters off Molokai.[206] According to reports from Hawaii News Now[207] and findings by the National Transportation Safety Board (NTSB), the aircraft experienced a loss of engine power shortly after takeoff. They were forced to ditch in the ocean.

News accounts highlighted several unusual circumstances. Director Fuddy was reportedly wearing an infant life vest, and investigators later stated that only one of its carbon dioxide cartridges was functioning while the other was punctured and empty. Witnesses described her as fearful and hyperventilating prior to losing consciousness. An autopsy concluded that her cause of death was acute cardiac arrhythmia brought on by stress and hyperventilation.

Although official reports attributed the incident to mechanical failure and medical factors, the timing of Director Fuddy's death, occurring amid ongoing legal challenges, public inquiries, and persistent controversy regarding the birth certificate, drew heightened attention from observers who had been closely following developments. For many, the episode underscored the intensity of the national debate and the unanswered questions that continued to surround the issue.

Whether viewed as a coincidence or as part of a broader sequence of events, Director Fuddy's death marked a moment that further deepened public interest and speculation at a time when demands for transparency were at their peak.

In March 2012, Maricopa County, Arizona, Sheriff Joe Arpaio announced that his office had conducted a six-month investigation into documents related to President Barack Obama's citizenship. According to Arpaio, the inquiry began after members of a Tea

---

206 "Hawaii Health Director Loretta Fuddy Killed in Plane Crash Off of Molokai," Civil Beat, December 12, 2013, https://www.civilbeat.org/2013/12/20648-hawaii-health-director-loretta-fuddy-killed-in-plane-crash-off-of-molokai/

207 Jennifer Sinco Kelleher, "Hawaii Official Killed in Plane Crash Remembered," Hawaii News Now, December 12, 2013, https://www.hawaiinewsnow.com/story/24209892/fuddy-remembered-for-role-in-hawaii-public-health/

Party organization submitted a petition in August 2011 requesting that the sheriff examine questions surrounding the authenticity of the birth certificate released by the Obama administration in 2011. During a news conference, Arpaio stated that investigators believed the digital image of the long-form birth certificate might have been electronically altered and that additional investigation was warranted to determine whether any forgery or fraud had occurred. The inquiry was conducted by the sheriff's volunteer "Cold Case Posse," a group composed of former law-enforcement officers and attorneys who assist the department without cost to taxpayers.[208]

Subsequent developments also extended the investigation into Obama's birth records. In 2014, reports circulated that Sheriff Joe Arpaio had opened a second criminal investigation[209] related to the digital image of the Certificate of Live Birth released by the White House in April 2011. According to statements attributed to lead investigator Mike Zullo, the renewed inquiry involved staff investigators rather than the volunteer "Cold Case Posse" that had conducted the earlier review. The investigation was described as focusing on whether additional evidence had emerged concerning the authenticity of the document posted on the White House website.

After a long five-year investigation, Sheriff Joe Arpaio made an announcement regarding the findings of the Cold Case Posse's complete, comprehensive analysis[210] of Barack Obama's birth certificate and related records.

According to Sheriff Arpaio and the investigators involved, the birth certificate posted by President Obama, along with the Selective Service registration, was determined by multiple experts consulted during the investigation to exhibit indicators of fraud. The

208 Kharli Mandeville, "Arpaio investigates Obama citizenship," The State Press, Mar. 1, 2012, https://www.statepress.com/article/2012/03/arpaio-investigates-obama-citizenship

209 "Arpaio's New Obama Investigation Now A Criminal One!" https://le.utah.gov/publicweb/MCKELMK/PublicWeb/43793/43793.html

210 Garrett Papit, "Comprehensive Analysis of Obama's Long Form Birth Certificate Acrobat File PDF," Scribd document, https://www.scribd.com/doc/100441711

Cold Case Posse's investigation spanned approximately five years, culminating in the release of its Complete Comprehensive Analysis on December 15, 2016, which concluded that the document was not authentic.

A video of Sheriff Arpaio discussing the findings is available online.[211]

According to the investigators, the file contains multiple layers that are inconsistent with what would be expected from a straightforward scan of a paper document. The analysis asserts that the layered structure cannot be explained by ordinary scanning, standard optimization, or routine file processing. Instead, it concludes that the characteristics observed, including isolated text layers, segmentation of form lines, color inconsistencies, and the presence of a "white halo" effect, are indicative of manual manipulation or assembly within the digital file.

The report further states that the object code within the PDF does not match what would typically be produced by an optimized scan, noting that the number and structure of layers differ materially from expected outputs. In addition, the analysis raises concerns regarding the document's digital chain of custody, observing that metadata appears to have been altered or removed, making it difficult to determine the precise sequence of processes used to create the final file.

Based on these findings, the report concludes that scanning and optimization alone cannot account for the anomalies observed in the document and suggests that the file may have been altered or constructed using additional software processes.

The preceding chapters have examined the historical and constitutional foundations of citizenship as understood by the generation that framed and ratified the Constitution. Their concern with allegiance, sovereignty, and the qualifications for public office was neither abstract nor theoretical; it reflected a deliberate effort to

211 "Sheriff Joe Arpaio Press Conference on Obama Birth Certificate Investigation," YouTube video, December 15, 2016, https://www.youtube.com/watch?v=jk3KRxTfkLM

safeguard the stability and independence of the new republic.

The requirement that the President be a "natural-born citizen" was included with particular care. The Founders, mindful of the vulnerabilities that had affected earlier nations, recognized that the office of Commander in Chief demanded undivided loyalty to the United States. Their understanding was shaped by the political philosophy of the time, the lessons of history, and a commitment to preserving self-government against both foreign influence and domestic faction.

Constitutional provisions endure not merely as historical artifacts, but as guiding principles intended to inform the conduct of public affairs across generations. For that reason, the study of original meaning is not an exercise in antiquarian interest; it is essential to maintaining continuity with the constitutional order as it was designed.

As I continued to examine the historical sources, including early legal commentaries, the debates of the founding era, and subsequent interpretations, it became increasingly apparent that questions concerning citizenship and eligibility have not remained confined to the past. Rather, they have periodically resurfaced in moments when public confidence in institutional processes has been tested.

The emergence of modern controversies surrounding presidential eligibility brought these issues into renewed focus. Such controversies, whatever one's conclusions about them, present an opportunity to consider how constitutional principles are applied in practice and how institutions respond when questions arise concerning the qualifications for high office.

My decision to examine contemporary developments grew out of this recognition. If constitutional provisions are to retain their force, they must be understood not only in their historical context but also in their present application. The transition from historical analysis to contemporary inquiry, therefore, reflects a continuation of the same question: how the constitutional framework operates when confronted with real-world circumstances.

In approaching these matters, I have sought to rely upon documentary records, publicly available sources, and the procedural history of relevant events. The aim is not to revisit past debates for their own sake, but to understand how enduring constitutional principles interact with modern institutions, including courts, administrative agencies, and the broader public discourse.

It is important to note that constitutional inquiry benefits from careful attention to both history and process. The American constitutional system rests upon the premise that questions of law are to be examined deliberately, with respect for precedent, institutional roles, and the rule of law. Examining contemporary controversies through this lens allows for a more complete understanding of how the system functions in practice.

The next chapter, therefore, turns to the contemporary record. They trace the development of public debate, the responses of governmental institutions, and the broader conversation that emerged as questions of citizenship and eligibility entered national discourse. In doing so, they seek to illuminate not only the events themselves but also the constitutional principles that frame them.

The transition from theory to application reflects a longstanding tradition within American constitutional thought: that principles articulated at the nation's founding must continually be examined in light of present circumstances. By considering both the historical foundations and the modern record, we may better appreciate the enduring relevance of the constitutional framework and the responsibilities it imposes upon citizens and institutions alike.

As the research deepened, what began as an intellectual inquiry gradually became something more personal. The questions I encountered were no longer confined to academic discussion or historical curiosity; they touched directly on the functioning of institutions I had long trusted and on principles I believed were foundational to the constitutional order.

At first, I assumed that if legitimate questions existed, they would be addressed through ordinary channels. Courts, public officials, and the press, I believed, would examine the issues carefully and provide clarity where needed. Yet as time passed, I observed what appeared to be a consistent reluctance to engage in the underlying constitutional questions directly. Filings were dismissed on procedural grounds, public debate often focused on personalities rather than legal principles, and opportunities for substantive examination seemed too narrow.

This experience created a growing sense of responsibility. If the constitutional framework depends upon citizens as well as institutions, then remaining a passive observer no longer feels sufficient. The matter had moved beyond abstract concern; it had become, in my view, a question of civic duty.

The decision to pursue legal action was not made lightly. Litigation carries financial, personal, and reputational costs, and I was fully aware that raising controversial constitutional questions could invite criticism or misunderstanding. Nevertheless, I believed that seeking judicial review represented the most appropriate avenue for resolving disputes of this nature within the rule of law.

By the time my case entered the courts, my purpose was straightforward: to ask whether the constitutional requirements for the presidency had been properly examined and to seek clarity through lawful means. Regardless of outcome, I felt compelled to ensure that the questions were at least presented within the institutional framework designed to address them.

It is from this sense of obligation, rather than from any desire for conflict, that the legal journey described in the following chapter began.

With these considerations in mind, we proceed with the contemporary developments that have brought renewed attention to the questions examined throughout this work.

I should also explain why I devote so much attention to the question of Barack Obama's eligibility. For me, the issue is not merely academic or political; it is deeply personal. During the implementation of the Affordable Care Act, my family experienced severe financial hardship. Before Obamacare, our health insurance cost approximately $3,000 per year. After its implementation, our premiums increased to more than $11,000 annually. We had insurance coverage that we valued and wanted to keep, but the rising costs eventually made it unaffordable. As a result, we were forced to cancel our coverage and go without insurance altogether. To make matters worse, during the years when the individual mandate was in effect, we were also required to pay a penalty for not maintaining coverage.

These experiences profoundly shaped my interest in constitutional government and the importance of adhering to the requirements set forth in the Constitution. My purpose in writing this book is not to attack any individual personally, but to examine what I believe are important constitutional questions that deserve serious consideration. My hope is that the evidence presented in these pages will encourage readers, scholars, public officials, and members of the judiciary to take a fresh and honest look at the constitutional issues surrounding presidential eligibility. If the conclusions advanced in this book are ultimately found to be correct, then I believe the legal consequences should be addressed according to the rule of law, however difficult or far-reaching those consequences may be. More than anything, I hope this work contributes to a renewed commitment to constitutional fidelity and the principle that no person is above the Constitution.

Readers interested in reviewing the extensive litigation surrounding President Obama's eligibility may consult independent compilations of the cases and administrative proceedings that arose during this period. These collections document the numerous challenges filed in federal courts, state courts, and administrative tribunals, as well as the decisions that followed. While this book discusses a number of the more significant cases, a more comprehensive listing can be found online at the following location:

https://www.scribd.com/document/118087031/Score-Card

The purpose of referencing this material is not to suggest that the volume of litigation alone proves any particular conclusion. Rather, it demonstrates the extent to which questions regarding presidential eligibility generated public interest, legal challenges, and judicial review throughout the Obama presidency.

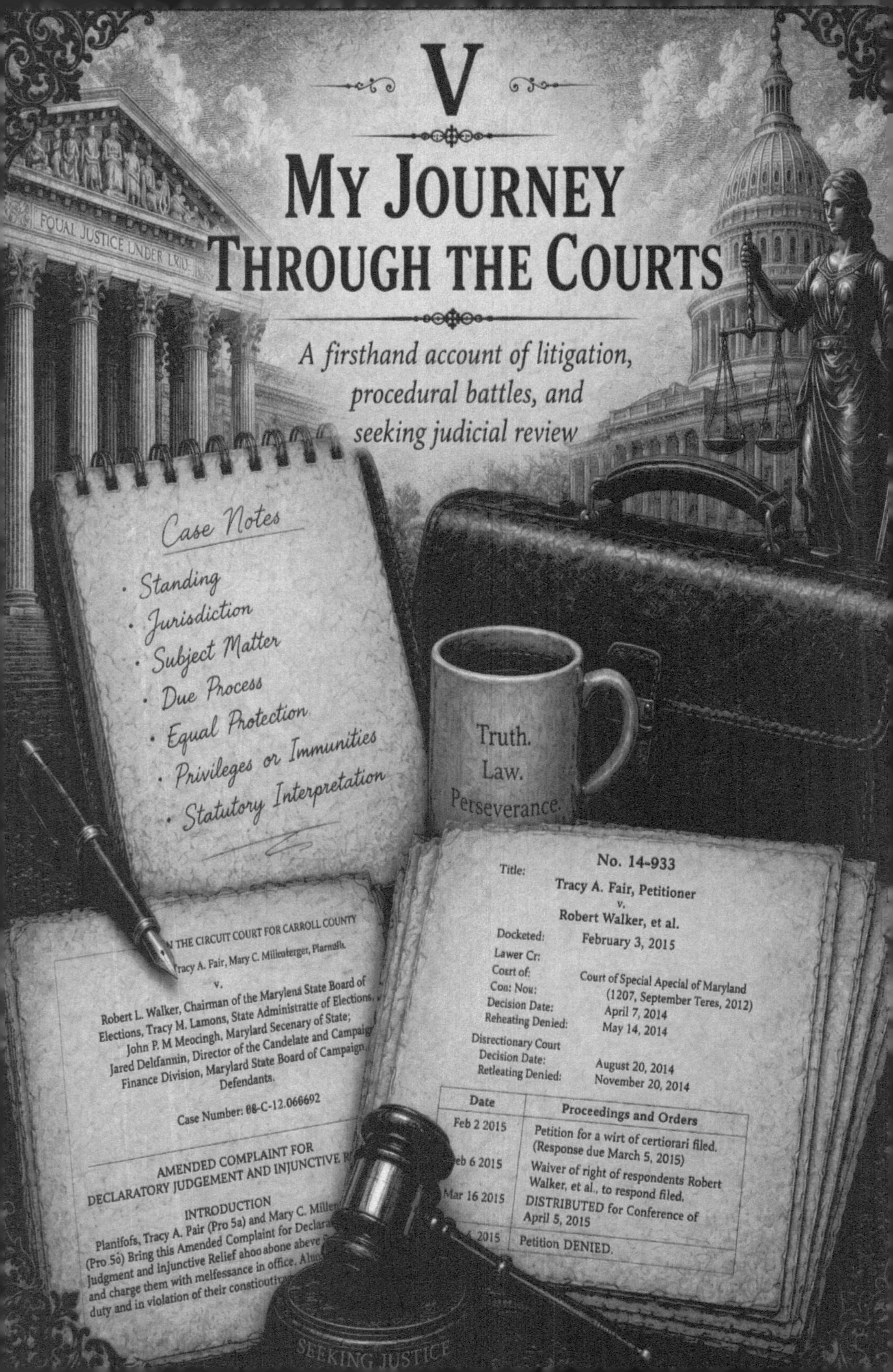
V
My Journey Through the Courts
A firsthand account of litigation, procedural battles, and seeking judicial review
EQUAL JUSTICE UNDER LAW
Case Notes
· Standing
· Jurisdiction
· Subject Matter
· Due Process
· Equal Protection
· Privileges or Immunities
· Statutory Interpretation
Truth.
Law.
Perseverance.
IN THE CIRCUIT COURT FOR CARROLL COUNTY
Tracy A. Fair, Mary C. Millenberger, Plaintiffs,
v.
Robert L. Walker, Chairman of the Marylena State Board of Elections, Tracy M. Lamons, State Administratte of Elections, John P. M Meocingh, Marylard Secenary of State; Jared Deldfannin, Director of the Candelate and Campaign Finance Division, Marylard State Board of Campaign, Defendants.
Case Number: 06-C-12.066692
AMENDED COMPLAINT FOR DECLARATORY JUDGEMENT AND INJUNCTIVE RELIEF
INTRODUCTION
Planifofs, Tracy A. Pair (Pro 5a) and Mary C. Mille (Pro 5ö) Bring this Amended Complaint for Declara Judgment and injunctive Relief ahoo abone abeve and charge them with melfessance in office. Alu duty and in violation of their constioutiv
No. 14-933
Title: Tracy A. Fair, Petitioner v. Robert Walker, et al.
Docketed: February 3, 2015
Lawer Cr:
Court of: Court of Special Apecial of Maryland
Con: Nou: (1207, September Teres, 2012)
Decision Date: April 7, 2014
Reheating Denied: May 14, 2014
Disrectionary Court Decision Date: August 20, 2014
Retleating Denied: November 20, 2014
Date | Proceedings and Orders
Feb 2 2015 | Petition for a wirt of certiorari filed. (Response due March 5, 2015)
Feb 6 2015 | Waiver of right of respondents Robert Walker, et al., to respond filed.
Mar 16 2015 | DISTRIBUTED for Conference of April 5, 2015
2015 | Petition DENIED.
SEEKING JUSTICE

V

My Journey Through the Courts

A firsthand account of litigation, procedural battles, and seeking judicial review

THE OBAMA ELIGIBILITY CASE FILINGS/ PROCEEDINGS

By the time the questions surrounding presidential eligibility reached the courts, I had already spent years researching the historical meaning of the Constitution's "natural-born Citizen" requirement. The controversies discussed in the previous chapters ultimately led me to pursue legal remedies, not as a political exercise, but to obtain judicial clarification of a constitutional provision I believed had been misunderstood or left unresolved. What followed was a series of legal filings and proceedings that brought these questions before multiple courts.

As these questions unfolded, it became increasingly clear to me that the issues involved were not merely academic or political disagreements. At their core lay fundamental questions about how constitutional requirements are interpreted, enforced, and understood within the institutions entrusted with upholding them.

If constitutional provisions can be set aside or left unresolved when they become difficult or controversial, the implications extend far beyond any single officeholder. Public confidence in the rule of law depends upon the belief that constitutional standards are applied consistently and transparently, particularly at the highest levels of government.

At the same time, pursuing these questions carried its own challenges. Raising constitutional concerns in public forums often brought skepticism, criticism, and, at times, outright dismissal. Engaging the issue required navigating legal complexities, institutional resistance, and the practical burdens associated with litigation, research, and public scrutiny.

For me, the matter was not simply about resolving a particular controversy, but about understanding whether the constitutional framework operates as intended when confronted with difficult questions. The experience underscored how institutional processes, public perception, and individual conviction can intersect in ways that test both perseverance and principle.

It is within this context, shaped by both the perceived importance of the questions and the obstacles encountered along the way, that the events described in the following chapter unfolded.

In 2012, I brought this evidence forward through the court system, ultimately seeking review by the Supreme Court. At no point during those proceedings was the evidence permitted to be heard. Instead, each court affirmed dismissal on procedural grounds. I overcame issues of standing, jurisdiction, and every other threshold requirement raised, yet when no substantive basis remained to deny review, the courts relied on the doctrine of laches.

Laches is a doctrine asserting that a claim was not brought within an appropriate time.[212] However, each of my filings were time-stamped by the court and demonstrates that the case was filed within the applicable periods. I communicated directly with the Maryland Board of Elections and the Secretary of State to confirm filing requirements and complied with those timelines accordingly.

---

212 Black's Law Dictionary, 11th ed., s.v. "laches."

It took three long years for my Obama eligibility case to reach the Supreme Court. In 2015, the Court denied my Petition for Certiorari,[213] confirming, in my view, the judiciary's unwillingness to address the constitutional qualifications for the presidency on the merits.

I am aware of numerous other litigants who filed similar actions during the same period, and like mine, their cases were dismissed without consideration of the underlying evidence. The shared objective among us was straightforward: to obtain clarity and ensure adherence to the Constitution in the selection of the Commander in Chief.

My case began with a filing in the Circuit Court for Carroll County, Maryland,[214] challenging the placement of Barack Obama on the ballot. The litigation ultimately culminated in my Petition for Writ of Certiorari before the Supreme Court of the United States.

The following documents reflect the progression of that litigation from its inception through final review.

My complete list of case filings is set forth below, beginning with the Supreme Court's final action. Each entry reflects a step in the procedural history of the litigation and documents the case's progression through multiple levels of review.

Fair v. Walker — Petition for Certiorari[215] DENIED by the Supreme Court (April 6, 2015)

This docket entry reflects the Supreme Court's decision not to grant review, effectively ending the litigation without addressing the underlying constitutional questions raised in the petition.

---

213 *Fair v. Walker*, No. 14-933, https://www.supremecourt.gov/search.aspx?filename=/docketfiles/14-933.htm

214 *Fair v. Walker* et al., Amended Complaint for Declaratory Judgment and Injunctive Relief, Circuit Court for Carroll County, Maryland, filed Mar. 23, 2012 reproduced at https://www.scribd.com/document/86426592/Maryland-Ballot-Challenge-Petition-to-remove-Obama-from-the-ballot

215 *Fair v. Walker*, Supreme Court Petition for Certiorari https://www.supremecourt.gov/search.aspx?filename=/docketfiles/14-933.htm

Supreme Court Petition for Certiorari[216] — Filed February 2, 2015.

This filing formally requested that the Supreme Court review the lower court decisions and consider the issues presented regarding ballot eligibility and constitutional qualifications.

Maryland Court of Appeals Denies Eligibility Petition[217] — Decided November 20, 2014

The state's highest court declined relief, leaving in place prior rulings and narrowing the remaining avenues for review.

Petitioner's Reply to Respondent's Answer[218] — Filed July 3, 2014

This reply addressed the respondents' arguments and clarified the petitioner's position on procedural and constitutional issues.

Respondent's Answer to Writ of Certiorari[219] — Filed June 16, 2014

The respondents set forth their opposition to the review, arguing that the petition should not proceed.

Petition for Writ of Certiorari in the Maryland Court of Appeals[220] — Filed May 29, 2014

This filing sought discretionary review following adverse rulings in lower courts.

Appendix for Petition for Writ of Certiorari[221] — Filed May 29,

216 *Fair v. Walker,* Supreme Court Petition for Certiorari https://www.supremecourt.gov/search.aspx?filename=/docketfiles/14-933.htm

217 *Fair v. Walker,* Maryland Court of Appeals https://docs.google.com/document/d/1bBk3H3tjsgWUv0WPHK3uPQPO3_nPMCAunUbhL2PRtYw/edit

218 *Fair v. Walker,* Petitioner's Reply to Respondent's Answer https://docs.google.com/file/d/0B1LGLpWgqgYFQ2ZENFpya2JzNzg/edit

219 *Fair v. Walker* Respondent's Answer to Writ of Certiorari https://docs.google.com/file/d/0B1LGLpWgqgYFblJ0YkhlZmRBb1U/edit?resourcekey=0-M_XKKxCHWjfUHlrQQCkGCQ

220 *Fair v. Walker* Petition for Writ of Certiorari https://docs.google.com/file/d/0B1LGLpWgqgYFNVBuR0Vua21ZakE/edit

221 *Fair v. Walker,* Appendix to Petition for Writ of Certiorari https://docs.google.com/file/d/0B1LGLpWgqgYFcjlUcjFGMm5ISEk/edit

2014

The appendix compiled relevant documents, orders, and supporting materials for judicial consideration.

Motion to Exceed Page Limitation[222] — Filed May 29, 2014

This motion requested permission to present a more detailed argument than ordinarily allowed.

Request for Judicial Notice[223] — Filed May 29, 2014

The petitioner asked the court to formally recognize certain facts and records relevant to the case.

Motion to Reconsider[224] — Filed May 7, 2014

This filing requested reconsideration of prior rulings believed to be in error.

Appellate Decision[225] (3-Judge Panel Hearing September 2013; Decided April 7, 2014)

The appellate court affirmed dismissal following review of the record.

Appellee's Reply Brief[226] — Filed June 3, 2013

This brief responded to arguments raised on appeal.

Appellate Brief[227] — Filed May 2013

---

222 *Fair v. Walker,* Motion to Exceed Page Limitation https://docs.google.com/file/d/0B1LGLpWgqgYFYUN4SWlyaGZzakE/edit

223 *Fair v. Walker,* Request for Judicial Notice https://docs.google.com/file/d/0B1LGLpWgqgYFMENfbmJ1ZDZmMlU/edit

224 *Fair v. Walker,* Motion to Reconsider, https://web.archive.org/web/20160831055917/http://www.unslaveamerica.com/wp-content/uploads/2014/04/Fair-v.-Obama-Motion-to-Reconsider.pdf

225 *Fair v. Walker,* Appellate Decision, (3-judge panel) https://web.archive.org/web/20210222180045/https://www.unslaveamerica.com/fair-v-walker-obama-appellate-decision

226 *Fair v. Walker,* Appellee's Reply Brief https://docs.google.com/file/d/0B1LGLpWgqgYFVjJmSXJDeEgzOWM/edit

227 *Fair v. Walker,* Appellate Brief https://www.scribd.com/document/135903907/Appellate-Brief-Fair-v-Obama-Walker

The opening appellate submission set forth legal grounds for reversal.

Maryland Obama Ballot Challenge Decision[228] — August 17, 2012

The trial court issued its decision regarding the ballot challenge.

Plaintiff's Opposition to Motion to Dismiss, Filed May 15, 2012[229]

This filing contested the defendants' attempt to terminate the case at an early stage.

Defendant's Motion to Dismiss[230] — Filed April 27, 2012

The defendants argued that the case should be dismissed on procedural and jurisdictional grounds.

Amended Complaint[231] — Filed March 23, 2012

The amended complaint clarified claims and refined the legal arguments.

Initial Ballot Challenge Petition[232] — Filed March 19, 2012

This filing initiated the challenge in state court.

Maryland Board of Elections Meeting Minutes[233] — September 27, 2012

The minutes reflect official discussion referencing the Obama

228 *Fair v. Walker*, Decision of Circuit Court for Carroll County https://docs.google.com/document/d/1wKKiOvnt0lMp6-qpjJyQxVuqE7PZwcPAihzA2dKtP-M/edit

229 *Fair v. Walker*, Plaintiff's Opposition to Motion to Dismiss, https://docs.google.com/document/d/1YNBrK5kRUyjBp_ek3XwgpzuJCnG46QN8uLBFN-FXLi0/edit

230 *Fair v. Walker*, Plaintiff's Opposition to Motion to Dismiss, https://docs.google.com/document/d/1YNBrK5kRUyjBp_ek3XwgpzuJCnG46QN8uLBFN-FXLi0/edit

231 *Fair v. Walker*, Amended Complaint https://www.scribd.com/document/86426592/Maryland-Ballot-Challenge-Petition-to-remove-Obama-from-the-ballot

232 *Fair v. Walker*, Petition to Remove Obama from the Ballot https://web.archive.org/web/20131212050804/http://www.scribd.com/doc/86426592/Maryland-Ballot-Challenge-Petition-to-remove-Obama-from-the-ballot

233 MD State Board of Elections, Meeting Minutes, 9/27/2012 https://elections.maryland.gov/pdf/minutes/2012_09.pdf

eligibility case.

Throughout the proceedings, courts repeatedly relied on procedural doctrines, most notably standing or laches, to decline review. In practical terms, laches meant the courts determined that the claims should not proceed due to timing considerations rather than reaching the substance of the issues raised. From my perspective, this procedural focus prevented a merits hearing despite the extensive record developed over several years.

Numerous litigants across the country pursued similar actions during this period, and many encountered comparable procedural outcomes. The shared objective among these efforts was to seek judicial clarity regarding constitutional requirements and to ensure that election processes were conducted in accordance with governing law.

The experience left a lasting impression on me regarding the challenges of litigating complex constitutional questions within the procedural framework of the courts. Regardless of differing viewpoints on the merits, the process itself illustrates how threshold doctrines can shape the course of litigation.

In 2017, better late than never, the American Journal of Legal History published an article entitled "The Reception of Vattel's Law of Nations in the American Colonies: From James Otis and John Adams to the Declaration of Independence."[234] This scholarship further confirms what this book has documented: that the Founders understood citizenship through the lens of natural law and allegiance, and that these principles were foundational to the constitutional framework they established.

From my perspective, the evidence presented throughout this work demonstrates that Barack Obama was never a legitimate president, but instead, was one who held office without meeting

---

234 William Ossipow and Dominik Gerber, "The Reception of Vattel's *Law of Nations* in the American Colonies: From James Otis and John Adams to the Declaration of Independence," American Journal of Legal History 57, no. 4 (December 2017): 521–555, https://doi.org/10.1093/ajlh/njx023

the constitutional qualifications required under Article II.[235] If the Constitution is to remain the supreme law of the land, then actions taken under an ineligible presidency raise serious questions that cannot simply be ignored.

We have assembled the historical record, the legal arguments, and the documentary evidence. The American people must confront what it means when constitutional requirements are not enforced. The responsibility now falls on citizens and public officials alike to restore fidelity to the rule of law and to ensure that constitutional standards for citizenship and eligibility are upheld.

It is deeply troubling to consider the political, institutional, and financial consequences that flowed from these events. Beyond policy decisions, the controversy has strained public trust, divided communities, and altered relationships among friends, families, and political allies. The long shadow of these disputes continues to shape public discourse.

Whether one agrees with the conclusions reached in this book or not, the questions presented herein deserve to be examined on their merits rather than dismissed through political convenience or public pressure. The evidence has been assembled, the arguments have been made, and the historical record has been placed before the reader. What remains is for those entrusted with preserving the Constitution—including elected officials, judges, and ultimately the American people—to determine whether these questions warrant further review and consideration. If constitutional government is to endure, then no office, no institution, and no individual can be placed beyond constitutional scrutiny. The Constitution must remain the final authority, and its requirements must be applied faithfully, consistently, and without exception.

THE END

235 U.S. Const. art. II, § 1, cl. 5.

About the Author

Tracy Fair, writing under the pen name Lexi Fehr, is an author and independent researcher with a longstanding interest in American history, constitutional law, and the foundations of citizenship.

For more than eighteen years, Tracy researched the historical, legal, and constitutional foundations of presidential eligibility and the meaning of the Constitution's "natural-born Citizen" requirement. This investigation included the examination of primary historical sources, congressional records, judicial opinions, diplomatic correspondence, and the writings of the Founding generation.

As part of that effort, Tracy pursued litigation challenging presidential ballot eligibility issues, including a lawsuit against the Maryland State Board of Elections that ultimately petitioned the Supreme Court of the United States. The research presented in this book reflects years of independent investigation into citizenship, allegiance, natural law, and the constitutional principles that shaped the American Republic.

In addition to her written research, Tracy is a video creator and editor who has produced more than 200 videos on the YouTube channel @KenyanBornObamAcorn, exploring constitutional issues, presidential eligibility, citizenship, and government accountability.

A constitutional advocate and lifelong student of history, Tracy resides in Maryland and is the proud parent of three grown children and grandmother of two granddaughters. This is her first published book.

www.ingramcontent.com/pod-product-compliance
Lightning Source LLC
LaVergne TN
LVHW090353240926
848801LV00001B/23
* 9 7 9 8 9 5 0 5 7 7 4 3 7 *